# DIVING INTO C

*a first course*

CW01080657

# DIVING INTO C
## *a first course*

*Terry Marris*

A member of the Hodder Headline Group
LONDON • SYDNEY • AUCKLAND

First published in Great Britain 1996 by
Arnold, a member of the Hodder Headline Group,
338 Euston Road, London NW1 3BH

*British Library Cataloguing in Publication Data*
A catalogue record for this book is available from the British Library

ISBN 0 340 65285 3

Produced by Gray Publishing, Tunbridge Wells, Kent
Printed and bound in Great Britain by J. W. Arrowsmith Ltd, Bristol

# Contents

# Preface

## Why choose this book?

This book is written for students following a first programming course. Such students may be on a BTEC Higher National course, or a National level course, taking GNVQ advanced in engineering or IT a GCE A-level course, or they may be just studying on their own. Those who wish to add another programming language to their repertoire will find this book useful.

The book is suitable for self-study. It can be used as the basis for a complete course, alone or to support a course of introductory lectures. The material can be covered in a 16-week course of lectures and practicals; in addition a major project could take another 16 weeks.

The teaching style is based on the premise that programming students learn best by example, so a tutorial approach is used. Small, simple programs introduce elements of the language and the fundamental programming concepts. Carefully graded exercises are used to reinforce understanding and to develop problem-solving skills. Everything the student needs to complete a substantial programming project is included: arrays, files, printer output, screen displays, documentation and guidance on writing a project report. One problem with the tutorial approach is that every feature of the language and the libraries cannot be discussed. However, on an introductory course the student does not need to know *everything* about the language in order to become a proficient programmer.

All the programs in the book may be found on the accompanying free disk. An ANSI C compiler is required to compile and run these programs.

## Why choose C as an introductory programming language?

It is perhaps the most popular language in use today. It is supported by an extensive standard library of routines which include a good range of input/output facilities. C supports modern program construction practice such as separate compilation of units, functional programming and abstract data types. It forms the basis of hybrid object orientated programming languages such as C++ and Objective C. And the diagnostics and type checking provided by recent C compilers help students (and working programmers) to write programs which are correct and robust.

By the time the student has completed this book, he or she should be ready to move on to advanced programming techniques.

*Terry Marris*

# Acknowledgements

The C language was devised by Dennis Ritchie and described in Kernighan, B. W. and Ritchie, D. M. *The C Programming Language*, Prentice-Hall, 1978, 1988. The American National Standards Institute (ANSI) together with the International Standards Organization (ISO) have formalised the language and library specifications. The material in this book is based on the ANSI C standard.

# 1

# Displaying Text

## 1.1 Introduction

C is a modern, general-purpose programming language created by Dennis Ritchie in the 1970s. It is used world-wide for a variety of applications. Examples of programs written in C include computer operating systems, company accounting systems and air-traffic control systems.

Many programs display something on the computer screen or monitor and our first program will do just this.

## 1.2 Displaying One Line of Text

The purpose of the first program in this chapter is to write

```
Good morning, sunshine.
```

on the screen. Here it is.

```
/* program 1.1 - displays a greeting on the screen. */
#include <stdio.h>
void main(void)
{
   printf("Good morning, sunshine.");
}
```

The line

```
/* program 1.1 - displays a greeting on the screen. */
```

is an example of a comment. A comment starts with /* and ends with */. A comment is written for the benefit of the person who has to read the program. The comment in this program tells us that the purpose of program 1.1 is to display a greeting on the screen. Another example of a comment is

```
/* Program written by: Terry Marris. */
/* Date written: 29 January 1994.    */
```

The next line in the program is

```
#include <stdio.h>
```

*stdio* is the name of a standard C library. This library provides a utility for writing text on the screen. An example of such a utility is the function named *printf*. We want to use this function so we specify that the contents of the library is to be included in our program. *stdio* stands for *st*andard *i*nput and *o*utput. An example of output is text displayed on a screen. An example of input is data entered via a keyboard. We shall deal with input later. The *h* in stdio.*h* stands for header because the library is always included near the head of a program. There are other libraries; we shall deal with them in due course. The *#* symbol is an essential part of the include command as are the angle brackets surrounding *stdio.h*.

The next line is

```
void main(void)
```

*main* is a compulsory part of every C program. *main* is the point where program execution starts. By program execution we mean that the instructions are carried out one after the other. In our program there is just one instruction; this is *printf("Good morning, sunshine.");*.

*void* means empty or nothing. In some circumstances, words other than *void* are used in connection with *main*. We shall discuss these words later. But for now, we shall use *void* as shown.

Now we come to the lines

```
{
    printf("Good morning, sunshine.");
}
```

Here, the braces *{* and *}* mark the beginning and end of a block. A block contains a sequence of instructions. Instructions are also known as statements. In our example there is only one statement: this is

```
printf("Good morning, sunshine.");
```

*printf* stands for *print* *f*ormatter. We use *printf* to arrange and print text on the screen. The text to be printed here is contained between the quotation marks. The quotation marks themselves are not printed on the screen when the statement is executed, that is, when the *printf* instruction is carried out.

There are some important points to note about C programs. C words such as *include*, *void* and *main* must be written entirely in small letters, that is, in lower case. Library function names such as *printf* must be written entirely in lower case with no spaces between the letters. Every statement must end with a semi-colon. Notice that a *semi-colon* follows the *printf* statement in program 1.1. And we follow the convention that a block of statements is indented by two spaces in from the left-hand margin. So, for example, using * to indicate one push of the spacebar, we write

```
{
**printf("Good morning, sunshine.");
}
```

## 1.3  Creating a Working Program

There are several steps to creating a working program. First, the program text has to be typed into the computer. An example of program text is program 1.1 shown above. A C program is entered with the aid of another program called an editor. An editor is usually provided as part of the C programming system. An editor allows you to create and correct program text.

Then the program text has to be translated into a code which enables the computer to perform the required tasks. The translation process is carried out by another program known as a C compiler. If the compiler finds, for example, an incorrectly written word or that a bracket is missing, it will fail to complete the translation process. If the compiler fails to complete the translation then a message indicating the error (or errors) is displayed on the screen. You should read these error messages before returning to the editor to correct the mistakes.

Then, when the translation has been successfully completed, the code has to be combined with code from libraries. These libraries contain functions which are responsible for managing devices such as a computer's screen. This process is achieved by yet another program known as a linker.

Finally, the completed program has to be loaded into the computer's memory and then executed.

Figure 1.1 summarises the steps required to create a working program.

The specific commands to edit, compile and link a program differ from one C programming system to another. So, unfortunately, such details cannot be given here; you will need to consult the manual which came with your C compiler.

### *Exercise 1.1*

1 Write and execute (that is, run) a program which will display, on the screen, the first line of a song or a poem. Use program 1.1 as a guide. You will need to pay careful attention to punctuation, to the way you use spaces and to the way you write C words such as *void*, *main* and *include*. C words are never written with capital letters.

2 A compile-time error occurs if the compiler fails to translate program text into

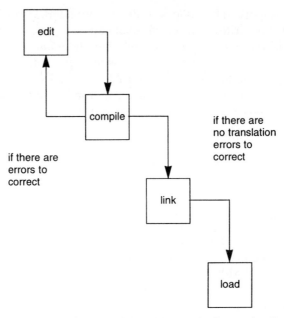

**Figure 1.1**   The steps required to complete and execute (i.e. run) a C program.

code. When a compile-time error occurs, a message known as a diagnostic is output on the screen. Diagnostics inform the programmer about the nature of the problem. Write down four compile-time error messages output by the compiler, the program line which caused each error and how each error could be corrected. Hint: you could introduce some deliberate errors in the program you wrote for question one above.

## 1.4   Displaying Several Lines of Text

The purpose of the second program in this chapter is to display on the screen

```
Good morning, sunshine.
The world says "Hello!".
```

We want to display *The world says "Hello!"*. on the next line below *Good morning, sunshine.*

To instruct our computer to place text on a new line we write

```
printf("\n");
```

The effect of this statement is to move the screen cursor to the beginning of the next line down. (A screen cursor is usually a flashing line or block which tells you where you are on the screen.) \n stands for the new-line character. Notice that \ is not the same thing as /. Here is a C program which prints two lines of text.

```
/* program 1.2 - displays two lines of text on the screen. */
#include <stdio.h>
void main(void)
{
  printf("Good morning, sunshine.");
  printf("\n");
  printf("The world says \"Hello!\".");
}
```

The line

```
printf("The world says \"Hello!\".");
```

prints *The world says "Hello!".* on the screen. If we want *printf* to print a quotation mark on the screen, then we write a backslash followed by a quotation mark like this: \".

Look at the block of statements bracketed between the *{* and the *}*; these statements are

```
printf("Good morning, sunshine.");
printf("\n");
printf("The world says \"Hello!\".");
```

We read the statement sequence like this:

```
do printf("Good morning, sunshine.");
and then do printf("\n");
and then do printf("The world says \"Hello!\".");
```

Notice that in program 1.2 the *printf* statements are written in line one under the other and that they are indented by two spaces in from the left-hand margin. We use indentation to help us to read and understand large and complex programs.

### Exercise 1.2

**1** Write and run a program which will display, on the screen, four lines of a song or a poem.

### 1.5 Writing Your Own Functions

The purpose of the next program is to display *MUM* on the screen. Each letter is to be made up from a pattern of asterisks. And each letter is to be displayed one under the other as shown in Figure 1.2.

We have already used the function *printf*. Now, we write some simple functions of our own.

**Figure 1.2**   Shows the output required from program 1.3.

The specification for writing *MUM* on the screen falls neatly into three parts: *write M*, *write U* and then *write M*. Each part can be written in the form of a function as shown in *writeM* below.

```
void writeM(void)
{
   printf(" *          * ");   printf("\n");
   printf(" **        ** ");   printf("\n");
   printf(" * *      * * ");   printf("\n");
   printf(" *    *    * ");     printf("\n");
   printf(" *          * ");   printf("\n");
   printf(" *          * ");   printf("\n");
   printf("\n");
}
```

Every function we write must be given a name. In this example, the name is *writeM*. Function names are also known as identifiers. Identifiers must not contain spaces or symbols such as & and -. We use the convention that an identifer chosen by ourselves always begins with a lower-case letter, and contains only lower-case letters except the first letter in a word; the first letter in a word is written in upper case. So, we prefer *writeM* to *writem* or *WRITEM* because it tells us that this is the name of a function. Notice that *void* is written before *writeM* and again in the brackets which follow *writeM*; the reasons for doing this will be explained later.

The function *writeM* contains a block of *printf* statements just as *main* does in program 1.2. In the function, two *printf* statements are written on each line (except the last one). Usually, we write each statement on its own line; this makes programs easier for us to read and understand. But in this case we have written two statements on each line to improve clarity.

Here is the complete program.

```
/* program 1.3 - displays MUM on the screen. */
#include <stdio.h>

void writeM(void);
void writeU(void);

void main(void)
{
  writeM();
  writeU();
  writeM();
}

void writeM(void)
{
  printf(" *        * ");  printf("\n");
  printf(" **      ** ");  printf("\n");
  printf(" * *    * * ");  printf("\n");
  printf(" *  **  * ");  printf("\n");
  printf(" *        * ");  printf("\n");
  printf(" *        * ");  printf("\n");
  printf("\n");
}

void writeU(void)
{
  printf(" *      * ");  printf("\n");
  printf(" *      * ");  printf("\n");
  printf(" *      * ");  printf("\n");
  printf(" *      * ");  printf("\n");
  printf("   *  *   ");  printf("\n");
  printf("    **    ");  printf("\n");
  printf("\n");
}
```

The two lines

```
void writeM(void);
void writeU(void);
```

are examples of function prototypes. A prototype makes known the name of a function to be used in the program. Every function must have its name declared in a prototype. The prototype for *printf* is found in *stdio.h*. That is why we write *#include <stdio.h>*. (Incidentally, notice the semi-colons which end each prototype.)

The main function

```
void main(void)
{
  writeM();
  writeU();
  writeM();
}
```

tells us that *writeM* is to be executed first, then *writeU* and then *writeM*; it specifies **what** is to be done and in which order.

The details of **how** the task is to be done is contained in each of the individual functions. For example, the details of how *writeM* works are written in the *writeM* function itself. Functions are used to minimise duplication of effort and to make large programs easier to read, understand and write.

Let us summarise the three main attributes of a function. A function has a prototype, for example:

```
void writeM(void);
```

A function is used or called upon to perform its task, for example

```
writeM();
```

A function has an implementation. An implementation contains details of how the function actually works. In C an implementation is known as a function definition. An example of a function definition is

```
void writeM(void)
{
  printf("  *         *  ");  printf("\n");
  printf("  **       **  ");  printf("\n");
  printf("  * *     * *  ");  printf("\n");
  printf("  *   * *   *  ");  printf("\n");
  printf("  *         *  ");  printf("\n");
  printf("  *         *  ");  printf("\n");
  printf("\n");
}
```

We illustrate all this in Figure 1.3.

```
/* program 1.3 - displays MUM on the screen. */

#include <stdio.h>


void writeM(void);
void writeU(void);


void main(void)
{
  writeM();
  writeU();
  writeM();
}


void writeM(void)
{
  printf(" *      * "); printf("\n");
  printf(" **    ** "); printf("\n");
  printf(" * *  * * "); printf("\n");
  printf(" * ** * "); printf("\n");
  printf(" *      * "); printf("\n");
  printf(" *      * "); printf("\n");
  printf("\n");
}

void writeU(void)
{
  printf(" *      * "); printf("\n");
  printf(" *      * "); printf("\n");
  printf(" *      * "); printf("\n");
  printf(" *      * "); printf("\n");
  printf("  *    *  "); printf("\n");
  printf("   **   "); printf("\n");
  printf("\n");
}
```

*function prototypes*

*function calls*

*function definition*

*function definition*

**Figure 1.3**  Function prototypes, calls and definitions.

## 1.6   Documentation

The purpose of documentation is to ensure a standard way of specifying and writing and describing programs. A standard way of working helps programmers to understand each others work. We shall adopt the following conventions.

Every program is to begin with comments which identifies the program, describes its purpose, names its author and states the date it was written or changed.

A space is to follow the character pair /* and precede */ to make the comments easy to read. For example

```
/* program 1.1 - displays a greeting. */
```

Always check that you end each comment correctly with */ and remember that you cannot have one comment inside another.

Programs are to be named in a systematic manner. An example of a systematic manner would be a two-letter code representing your course followed by your initials and a program number. Remember that names cannot contain spaces or symbols such as - and &.

A function's identifier is to be descriptive, that is, the function's purpose is to be obvious from its name. Function names are to be written in lower case except the first letter in each word (but not the first word) which makes up the name; these are to be written in upper case. This convention makes names readable and different from C words.

A block of statements sandwiched between a { and an } is to be indented by two spaces to help make the program structure clear to the (human) reader.

Every statement is to be written on a new line; the only exception to this is if several statements written on the same line makes the program easier to understand. Many statements written on the same line usually makes programs unnecessarily difficult to read and understand.

At least two blank lines are to separate one function from the next; this helps the reader to see where one function ends and the next one begins.

## 1.7   Programming Principles

Divide a program up into functions – each function should perform one small, specific task; this makes large programs easier to understand and change. The main function should define **what** tasks are to be done. Other functions should contain the details of **how** each task is to be carried out.

Pay strict attention to layout and to the naming of functions at the time the program is being entered or edited; this helps to minimise the chances of making errors and makes it easier for others (such as teachers!) to see your mistakes.

*Exercise 1.3*

**1** Write a program which will print your initials, one under the other, in large capital letters. The capital letters should be made up of asterisks and be eight character spaces wide and six lines high. Your program should use functions. Your initials should be displayed on the screen.

**2** Usually, the process of producing an executable program results in several files being saved on your disk directory. Examine your disk directory and write down the names of the files which were produced as a result of creating and running your first program. Explain the origin of each file. Use Figure 1.4 to help you.

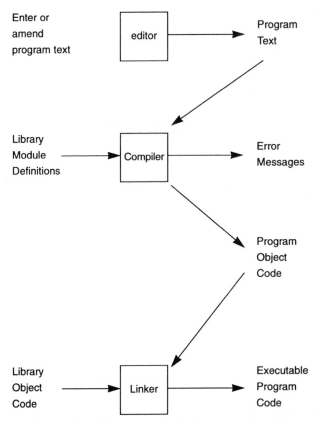

**Figure 1.4**   The edit–compile–link process to produce an executable program. The input to the compiler is program text (e.g. *prog1.c*) and library module definitions (e.g. *stdio.h*). The output from a compiler includes errors (if any) and object code (e.g. *prog1.o*). Object code is linked with library modules (e.g. *c.lib*) to form a complete and executable program (e.g. *prog1.exe*).

# 2

## Arithmetic

### 2.1 The Natural Numbers

We have all used natural counting numbers such as 1, 2 and 3 in simple arithmetic calculations. In C, the natural counting numbers between 0 and 65535 inclusive are known as *unsigned int* values. (*unsigned* because the values are never negative, *int* because they are integers, that is, whole numbers.)

Just as in ordinary arithmetic, we can add, subtract, multiply and divide *unsigned int* values. And we can find the remainder after dividing one *unsigned int* by another.

in normal arithmetic                    in C

$7 + 2 = 9$                              $7 + 2 == 9$
$7 - 2 = 5$                              $7 - 2 == 5$
$7 \times 2 = 14$                        $7 * 2 == 14$
$7 \div 2 = 3$ remainder 1               $7 / 2 == 3$
                                         $7 \% 2 == 1$

The two equal symbols $==$ together mean "is the same as", the $*$ means "multiply" and the $\%$ means "the remainder after division".

An *unsigned int* value can never be negative or less than zero. So, as far as *unsigned ints* are concerned, the expression $2 - 3$ has no meaning; $2 - 3$ cannot equal $-1$. Similarly, if the largest *unsigned int* is 65535, then the result of $65535 + 1$ cannot be an *unsigned int*. (With some C programming systems the largest *unsigned int* value may be more than 65535.) The result of any calculation involving *unsigned int* values must remain within the range from 0 up to 65535 if the answer is to be sensible.

Let us write a simple C program which will print the result of adding two *unsigned int* numbers.

```
/* program 2.1 - prints the sum of two numbers. */
#include <stdio.h>

void main(void)
{
   printf("%u", 7u + 2u);
   printf("\n");
}
```

The result of running this program is that 9 is displayed on the screen.

In ordinary arithmetic, we would write the number seven, for example, like this: 7. But in C we have to indicate that the number is an *unsigned int* value. We do this by attaching the letter *u* (or *U*) to the number thus: *7u*.

Now look at the *printf("%u", 7u + 2u)* statement. The *%u* specifies that the result of *7u + 2u* is to be printed in *unsigned* decimal format. In this context, decimal means base 10 – the base used for normal everyday arithmetic. And the format is the normal, everyday way in which positive whole numbers are written.

*%u* is an example of a conversion specification. A conversion specification specifies the format in which a value is to be shown on the screen. Notice that the conversion specification is enclosed within quotation marks.

We have seen the letter *u* used for two different purposes. First, it is used in a conversion specification. Second, it is used to specify that a number is an *unsigned int* value.

Program 2.1 is not particularly useful. The program has to be changed if it is to print the sum of two different numbers. This may not be a problem to people who are programmers. But people who use programs are not usually programmers. We cannot expect non-programmers to make changes to programs. So what we want the next program to do is

- allow the user to enter a number at the keyboard
- store the number in a suitable place in the computer's memory
- enter another number and store it in another location in memory
- sum the contents of these two stored values and display the result on the screen.

But first we follow a small but necessary diversion.

## 2.2  Variables

A computer's memory is perhaps best regarded as a store. Data, such as numbers, can be held in the store. Processes, such as arithmetic, can be applied to data held in the store.

The store comprises a sequence of storage locations. Each storage location is numbered from zero up to (say) 65535 and every location has its own number. The number which identifies a storage location is known as its address (see Figure 2.1).

A storage location is a container in which a value may be stored.

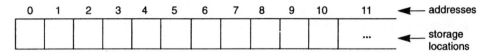

**Figure 2.1**   Store is a set of sequentially numbered storage locations.

Suppose the value 26 is held in the store. Then we can imagine a storage location at address 65508 say, which contains this value – see Figure 2.2.

**Figure 2.2**   A location in store contains a value.

A storage location can hold a value of a specified kind or type. An example of a type is an *unsigned int*. A value of type *unsigned int* is a whole number, either zero or positive. So, a value such as 3.1416 (which is not a whole number) cannot be stored in a location specified to hold an *unsigned int* value. A location in store designated to hold a value of some specified type is known as a variable. How can we define a variable in C? To define a variable which can store a value of type *unsigned int*, and to name it *aNumber*, we write

```
unsigned int aNumber;
```

At this point, the value stored in *aNumber* is not defined. But the address at which the variable is located is determined automatically by the C programming system (see Figure 2.3).

**Figure 2.3**   The contents of a variable are undefined – unless a value is explicitly stored there.

We could allocate a value, 28 say, to be stored in this variable by writing

```
unsigned int aNumber = 28u;
```

The symbol = is known as the assignment operator. It copies the value of whatever is written on its right into a variable written on its left. In our example, it places the value 28 into the variable *aNumber*. Now we can picture the variable as shown in Figure 2.4.

aNumber

```
┌────┐
│ 28 │
└────┘
```

**Figure 2.4**   The variable named *aNumber* contains the value 28.

Program 2.2 below prints the address at which the variable *aNumber* is located, together with the value it contains.

```
/* program 2.2 - displays the address at which a      */
/*               variable is located, together with   */
/*               the value stored at that address.    */

#include <stdio.h>

void main(void)
{
   unsigned int aNumber = 28u;

   printf("The variable is located at address %u",
                                               &aNumber);
   printf("\n");
   printf("It contains the value %u", aNumber);
   printf("\n");
}
```

The result of running this program on my computer system is that

```
The variable is located at address 65508
It contains the value 28
```

is displayed on the screen.

Every variable must be defined before it is used. And every variable must be given a name. A variable name is also known as an identifier. As mentioned in Chapter 1, identifiers must not contain spaces or symbols such as & and -. And again, we use the convention that identifiers chosen by ourselves always begin with a lower case letter and are always written entirely in lower case, except the first letter in a word – this is always written in upper case. In our example shown above, the variable identifier is *aNumber*. Any identifier chosen by ourselves should be descriptive, that is, its name should suggest its purpose. So, for example, the identifier *aNumber* is chosen because the variable's purpose is to store a number value.

The statement

```
printf("It contains the value %u", aNumber);
```

is straightforward. Even though the conversion specification *%u* is part of the text between the quotation marks, it is not printed (the % symbol sees to that). But the text *It contains the value* is printed.

The ampersand symbol in *&aNumber* specifies that the address at which the variable *aNumber* is located (and not its contents) is the value to be printed. And since an address is a positive number, the *%u* conversion specification is used. (Strictly, the conversion specification should be *%p* but this usually prints an address in hexadecimal format, which is not so easy to understand.)

## 2.3   Interactive Input

Program 2.1 – to display the result of adding two numbers – is limited because, in order to find the sum of a different pair of numbers we have to change the program. If a non-programmer was using our program, then it would be unreasonable to expect him or her to amend it. Our strategy now is to obtain input from the keyboard while the program is running. How can that be done?

First, we prompt the user with something like

```
printf("Please enter a number: ");
```

Then we read the keys pressed by the user and store them. Any key pressed on the keyboard generates a character. In C, a character is known as a *char*. To define a variable to store a sequence of characters we write

```
char string[BUFSIZ];
```

Here, *char* is a data type. *string* is a variable identifer chosen to suggest a sequence of characters – in computing, a sequence of characters is known as a string. *BUFSIZ* specifies the maximum number of characters to be stored. Its value, typically 512, is defined in *stdio.h*. To store the character values entered at the keyboard we write

```
gets(string);
```

*gets* gets a string of characters from the keyboard and places them in the named variable. Here, the named variable is *string*. *gets* waits for the user to press the return or enter key; this key indicates that there are no more characters to be entered. The characters may be letters of the alphabet, but in this case we expect them to be digits because we are dealing with numbers.

Finally, we convert the character digits into a single number in *unsigned int* format. This is achieved by the function *sscanf*. *sscanf* scans a string and converts its contents into a specified format. To convert the contents of *string* into *unsigned int* format, and to store the result in a variable named *aNumber* we write

```
sscanf(string, "%u", &aNumber);
```

The conversion specification, *%u*, is the same as the one used in the *printf* function. Notice the use of the address operator, *&*, which prefixes the variable's identifier; this is compulsory. Both *gets* and *sscanf* are defined in the *stdio* library.

We need to read natural numbers entered at the keyboard on different occasions for different purposes. So it would be handy if we wrote a single function to do the job in most circumstances. Here is one version of the function. (Do not worry if you find the function strange; functions are explained in more detail in Chapter 3. You do not need to understand the function fully in order to use it.)

```
unsigned unsignedNumberRead(void)
{
   char string[BUFSIZ];
   unsigned aNumber = 0u;

   printf("Number? ");
   gets(string);
   sscanf(string, "%u", &aNumber);
   return aNumber;
}
```

For example, given the variable definition

```
unsigned int ageInYears;
```

we can use the function to input a number from the keyboard by writing

```
ageInYears = unsignedNumberRead();
```

Let us look at some of the details not yet explained. The last statement in the function is

```
return aNumber;
```

The effect of this is to send the value stored in *aNumber* back to the point where the function was called. In our example shown above, this value is placed in the variable *ageInYears*. Here is another example:

```
unsigned numberOfStudentsInThisRoom;   ← variable definition

numberOfStudentsInThisRoom = unsignedNumberRead(); ← function
                                                       call
```

The value contained in the function's variable *aNumber* is returned and stored *in numberOfStudentsInThisRoom*.

The prompt *Number?* is perhaps not appropriate for every situation. Since we would like to use the same function but in different cirmcumstances, we want to be able to specify the prompt to suit the occasion. For example:

```
ageInYears = unsignedNumberRead("What is your age in years? ");
```

or

```
numberOfStudents = unsignedNumberRead("How many students? ");
```

Here, we have specified the required prompt at the point of call. Now we modify the function to match.

```
unsigned unsignedNumberRead(char prompt[])
{
   char string[BUFSIZ];
   unsigned aNumber = 0u;

   printf("%s", prompt);
   gets(string);
   sscanf(string, "%u", &aNumber);
   return aNumber;
}
```

The function heading is

```
unsigned unsignedNumberRead(char prompt[])
```

The C keyword word *int* has been dropped. The terms *unsigned int* and *unsigned* are synonyms – they are two different names for the same object. The function identifier is *unsignedNumberRead*. The function requires a string to be given to it. This is specified by the expression

```
char prompt[]
```

The maximum number of characters to be contained in the string variable *prompt* is not specified here; it is specified before the function is called. The function is supplied with a value to be stored in *prompt* at the point where the function is called. So, for example, if the function call is

```
ageInYears = unsignedNumberRead("What is your age in years? ");
```

then *prompt* would contain *What is your age in years?*.

The contents of *prompt* are displayed by the statement

```
printf("%s", prompt);
```

Here, the conversion specification is *%s*. The *s* specifies that the contents of *prompt* are to be printed in the format of a string, that is, as a sequence of characters.

Finally, we come to the program itself. The program, shown below, asks the user to enter two numbers. The program then displays the result of adding these two numbers together.

```
/* program 2.3 - inputs two numbers, outputs their sum. */

#include <stdio.h>

unsigned unsignedNumberRead(char []);


void main(void)
{
   unsigned aNumber, anotherNumber;

   aNumber = unsignedNumberRead("Number? ");
   anotherNumber = unsignedNumberRead("Another number? ");
   printf("Their sum is %u", aNumber + anotherNumber);
   printf("\n");
}

unsigned unsignedNumberRead(char prompt[])
{
   char string[BUFSIZ];
   unsigned aNumber = 0u;

   printf("%s", prompt);
   gets(string);
   sscanf(string, "%u", &aNumber);
   return aNumber;
}
```

An example of a program run is

```
Number? 3
Another number? 4
Their sum is 7
```

The values chosen and entered by the user are shown in bold type.

*Exercise 2.1*

**1** Run program 2.2, shown in section 2.2 above, on your computer system.
**2** Write a program to the following specification. The program is to ask the user to enter two numbers. The numbers entered should be stored in variables. Then the program should display the result of multiplying the two numbers together.
**3** Write a program which will print the result of dividing one number by another.
**4** Write a program which will print the remainder obtained after dividing one number by another. Remember that division involving unsigned int values always truncates, that is, cuts off, any fractional part. So, for example, 7 / 3 == 2 and 2 / 3 == 0.
**5** Write a program which will input a number of days and calculate and output the number of weeks and days it contains. For example, if the user entered 17 days, then the program should display 2 weeks 3 days. Hint: you could use days /7 to give you the number of weeks, and days % 7 to give you the number of days in the part week.

## 2.4   The Large Natural Numbers

The maximum value of type *unsigned int* is typically 65535, hardly big enough to deal with astronomical distances or figures involving millions of dollars or pounds. C provides the *unsigned long int* data type whose largest value is at least 4,294,967,295 that is, over four thousand million. The following program prints the largest value that can be stored in a variable of type *unsigned long int*.

```
/* program 2.4 - prints the largest unsigned long int value. */
#include <stdio.h>
#include <limits.h>

void main(void)
{
   printf("%lu", ULONG_MAX);
   printf("\n");
}
```

The value represented by *ULONG_MAX* (unsigned long maximum) is defined in *limits.h*. This value is printed by the line

```
printf("%lu", ULONG_MAX);
```

Here, the conversion specification is *%lu* for *long unsigned*. Notice that it is the letter *l* which follows the % symbol (and not the number 1).

The usual arithmetic operators, +, −, *, / and % can be used with values of type *unsigned long*. (*unsigned long* and *unsigned long int* mean the same thing.) Let us look at a simple example which uses values of type *unsigned long*.

Suppose that every week the area covered by green algae on a pond doubles in size. This week's algae population size is two times last week's. We express this by writing algaePopulationSize' = algaePopulationSize × 2

The expression means the current algaePopulationSize is equal to the previous algaePopulationSize times 2. Here, the prime symbol (') means the value after the calculation has taken place. The equivalent in C is

```
algaePopulationSize = algaePopulationSize * 2;
```

This means that the value of two times the old *algaePopulationSize* is assigned to, or stored in, *algaePopulationSize*; the old value is overwritten with the new value. Figure 2.5 illustrates the point.

**Figure 2.5**   Shows the contents of the variable before the calculation has taken place, and afterwards.

The following program inputs this week's area covered by algae and outputs the area which will be covered next week.

```
/* program 2.5 - calculates the new area of algae which */
/*               doubles in size every week.             */

#include <stdio.h>

unsigned long unsignedLongRead(char []);

void main(void)
{
   unsigned long algaePopSize;

   algaePopSize = unsignedLongRead(
                    "This weeks area covered by algae? ");
   algaePopSize = algaePopSize * 2ul;
   printf("The area covered next week will be %lu",
                                          algaePopSize);
   printf("\n");
}
```

```
unsigned long unsignedLongRead(char prompt[])
{
  char string[BUFSIZ];
  unsigned long aNumber = 0ul;

  printf("%s", prompt);
  gets(string);
  sscanf(string, "%lu", &aNumber);
  return aNumber;
}
```

An example of a program run is

```
This weeks area covered by algae? 64000
The area covered next week will be 128000
```

The function *unsignedLongRead* is much the same as the function *unsignedNumberRead* described in section 2.3 above, the essential difference being the line

```
sscanf(string, "%lu", &aNumber);
```

Here, the conversion specification is *%lu*, just as it is in the *printf* function.

Now, the conversion characters for values of type *unsigned long* is the letter *l* followed by *u*, but specific values of type *unsigned long* have the letters *ul* (or *UL*) attached to them – the order in which the letters are written is reversed. This is illustrated in the following example which prints the value of *128000ul*.

```
/* program 2.6 - prints an unsigned long constant value. */
#include <stdio.h>

void main(void)
{
  printf("%lu", 128000ul);
  printf("\n");
}
```

When run, this program prints

```
128000
```

on the screen.

Specific numeric values such as *128000ul* and *65000u* are known as constants.

*Exercise 2.2*

**1** Run program 2.4. Then amend the program so that it displays the value of
*UINT_MAX*. *UINT_MAX* represents the largest unsigned integer value on your
computer system; its value is defined in *limits.h*.

## 2.5   The Integers

Sometimes we need to use negative numbers. For example, a temperature of
−10 degrees celsius represents 10 degrees below zero or freezing point.

A whole number value between, typically, −32768 and +32767 is known in C as an
*int* value. *int* stands for integer; it means a whole number such as −3, −2, −1, 0, 1, 2, 3
and 4. An *int* constant does not have have a suffix (whereas *unsigned int* constants end
with u or U). The usual arithmetic operators +, − and * can be used with *int* values.
However, to divide or to find the remainder after division, we use the *div* function
defined in the *stdlib* library. We discuss this function in Appendix B. (We do not use
the / operator because, when negative values are used, the result is not the same for
every C programming system. For example, in ordinary arithmetic, 7 / −2 = −3.5. But
in C, the result might be either −3 or −4 depending on the compiler used. And again,
we do not use the % operator because, for example, 7 % −2 == 1 with some computer
systems, and 7 % −2 == −1 in others. However, knowing these problems, you could
use the divide and modulus operators with caution.)

Program 2.7 prints the least and the largest *int* value.

```
/* program 2.7 - prints the least and the largest int value. */

#include <stdio.h>
#include <limits.h>


void main(void)
{
   printf("Least int value is %d \n", INT_MIN);
   printf("largest int value is %d \n", INT_MAX);
}
```

Notice here that the newline character, \n, has been included with the text to be
displayed.

*%d* is the conversion specification for decimal (that is, base 10) integers. And *%d*
is used in the conversion of a string to an *int* value as shown in the function
*intNumberRead*.

```
int intNumberRead(char prompt[])
{
   char string[BUFSIZ];
   int aNumber = 0;
   printf("%s", prompt);
   gets(string);
   sscanf(string, "%d", &aNumber);
   return aNumber;
}
```

Just as we have *unsigned* and *unsigned long* data types, so we have the *long int* type. The largest *long int* value is represented by *LONG_MAX*. *LONG_MAX* is defined in *limits.h* and its value is, typically, 2,147,483,647. The value of *LONG_MIN* is usually –2,147,483,647. The conversion specifier for *long int* values is *%ld* (the letter *l* followed by *d*). And a *long int* constant ends with a letter *l* (or *L*), for example: *123456789L*. The terms *long int* and *long* have the same meaning.

### Exercise 2.3

**1** Write a program which will print the least and the largest *long int* value.
**2** Write a function named *longIntRead* which will input a number from the keyboard as a *long int*. Then write a program to test the function. Hint: you could use the *intNumberRead* function to guide you.

## 2.6   The Real Numbers

We use the *float* data type when we want to maintain some accuracy in calculations involving division, for example, when we want 2 divided by 3 to equal 0.666667 (and not 0). A constant value of type *float* contains a decimal point and the suffix *f* or *F*.

We use the *double* data type when we want even more accuracy in calculations, such as those that might be used for scientific purposes or for company accounting systems. *double* stands for *double* precision float.

The usual arithmetic operators, +, –, * and / can all be used with values of type *float* or *double*.

The following program, which features the *double* data type, asks the user to enter a number representing a value in degrees celsius, and then it calculates and outputs the corresponding value in degrees fahrenheit.

```
/* program 2.8 - converts a temperature in degrees celsius */
/*                into fahrenheit.                          */

#include <stdio.h>

double doubleNumberRead(char []);
```

```
void main(void)
{
   double celsius, fahrenheit;

   celsius = doubleNumberRead("Celsius? ");
   fahrenheit = 9.0 * celsius / 5.0 + 32.0;
   printf("Fahrenheit equivalent is %0.2f \n", fahrenheit);
}

double doubleNumberRead(char prompt[])
{
   char string[BUFSIZ];
   double aNumber = 0.0;

   printf("%s", prompt);
   gets(string);
   sscanf(string, "%lf", &aNumber);
   return aNumber;
}
```

An example of a program run is

```
Celsius? 36.9
Fahrenheit equivalent is 98.42
```

The variables *celsius* and *fahrenheit* are defined to be of type *double* in the line

```
   double celsius, fahrenheit;
```

The effect of the statement

```
   celsius = doubleNumberRead("Celsius? ");
```

is to place the value entered by the user into *celsius*. The next statement calculates the equivalent value in fahrenheit.

```
   fahrenheit = 9.0 * celsius / 5.0 + 32.0;
```

Notice that the constant values, namely 9.0, 5.0 and 32.0, all contain a decimal point (and no suffix). This identifies them as being constants of type *double*.
   The value stored in *fahrenheit* is displayed by the line

```
   printf("Fahrenheit equivalent is %0.2f \n", fahrenheit);
```

The conversion specification is *%0.2f*. It specifies that the value stored in *fahrenheit* is to be displayed with two digits after the decimal point. To display a *float* (or *double*) value with, say, four digits after the decimal point we would write %0.4f as the conversion specification. The number following the decimal point in the conversion specification specifies the number of digits to be printed after the decimal point.

Now look at the *sscanf* statement in the *doubleNumberRead* function.

```
sscanf(string, "%lf", &aNumber);
```

Here, the conversion specification is *%lf* (letter *l* followed by *f*). The letter *l* specifies that the value in string is to be converted to a *double* rather than a *float*. This conversion specification is not the same as the one used in *printf*; in *printf* we would use *%f* to print a *double* number value.

We can divide one double number by another and find the remainder by using the *fmod* function. For example, to find the remainder obtained when 7.00 is divided by 4.00

```
fmod(7.00, 4.00) == 3.00
```

*fmod* is defined in the math library.

We can divide one *double* number by another, to give an answer without a remainder and without a fractional decimal part, by using the *floor* function. For example

```
floor(7.00 / 4.00) == 1.00
```

The *floor* of a number of type *double* is the largest integer (expressed as a *double*) which is less than the number. For example,

```
floor(16.2) = 16.0, floor(16.8) = 16.0 and
floor(-16.2) = -17.0.
```

The following program shows how *fmod* and *floor* may be used.

```
/* program 2.9 - converts pence into pounds and pence. */
#include <stdio.h>
#include <math.h>

double doubleNumberRead(char prompt[]);

void main(void)
{
  double pounds, pence;

  pence = doubleNumberRead("Pence? ");
  pounds = floor(pence / 100.00);
  pence = fmod(pence, 100.00);
  printf("That is %0.0f pounds and %0.0f pence.\n", pounds, pence);
}
```

```
double doubleNumberRead(char prompt[])
{
   char string[BUFSIZ];
   double aNumber = 0.0;

   printf("%s", prompt);
   gets(string);
   sscanf(string, "%lf", &aNumber);
   return aNumber;
}
```

An example of a program run is

```
Pence? 204
That is 2 pounds and 4 pence.
```

## 2.7  Mixed Number Type Arithmetic

In each calculation shown so far, only variables and constants of the same type have been used. For example, in program 2.8 we find

```
fahrenheit = 9.0 * celsius / 5.0 + 32.0;
```

*fahrenheit* and *celsius* are variables of type *double*, and the constants *9.0, 5.0* and *32.0* are also of type *double*. This is not always convenient. We often want to use mixed number types in calculations. For example, suppose we want to calculate the number of times a heart beats in a lifetime. We multiply the number of times it beats in a minute by 60 to obtain the number of times it beats in an hour. We multiply the beats per hour by 24 to obtain the number of times it beats in a day. We multiply beats per day by 365.25 to obtain the number of times it beats in a year. (The 0.25 takes leap years into account.) We multiply beats per year by the number of years in a lifetime. The calculation involves *long unsigned ints*, *unsigned ints* and a *double* precision float.

```
beatsInALifetime = beatsPerMinute * 60u * 24u * 365.25 * years
   long unsigned         unsigned      unsigned   double unsigned
```

Each arithmetic type has an upper limit to the value that can be stored. If we list the arithmetic data types introduced so far in the order of their maximum values (largest first) we obtain the list shown in Figure 2.6 on the next page.

We can promote a value of a smaller type (lower down in the list) to a larger type value (higher up in the list) with no problem. For example, an *unsigned* value such as *56* can fit into a variable of type *double*; here, the value stored would be *56.0000000000*.

But if we demote a value of a larger type to a smaller type, then information is lost. For example, if we try to store a *double* value such as *38000.00* in an *int* variable then we loose information because the largest value that can be stored there is *32767*; in

| | |
|---|---|
| double | largest |
| float | |
| unsigned long | |
| unsigned | |
| int | smallest |

**Figure 2.6**   The relative sizes of the number types.

this example, we have no way of knowing exactly what value will be stored. And even if a *double* value was not too big to be stored in an *int* variable, the digits after the decimal point would be lost.

Looking at the calculation to work out the number of heartbeats in a lifetime, we can promote each *unsigned* value to *double* (to match the 365.25) so that the result of the calculation is a *double* value. But if we assign a *double* value to the *long unsigned* variable *beatsInALifetime* some accuracy in the result will be lost. In this case, we can live with the inaccuracy. But there may well be circumstances where such inaccuracy cannot be tolerated. A solution would be to perform all calculations using values of type *double*. But this wastes space in memory (a larger data type value requires more space for storage than a smaller one) and is not always convenient.

We can rely on C to automatically promote a smaller type value to a larger type in an arithmetic calculation. But we have to explicitly coerce a larger type value into a smaller type. We do this with a cast operator.

In the following example the cast operator is (*long unsigned*).

```
beatsInALifetime =
             (long unsigned)beatsPerMinute * 60U * 24U *
                                          365.25 * years;
```

A cast operator is a named type enclosed within brackets. It temporarily changes the type of the expression which follows it to the named type. Why should this be done? Because the presence of the double constant *365.25* causes the other terms to be promoted to *double* before the calculation takes place and we need to store the result of the calculation in a variable of type *unsigned long*.

Here is the complete program which inputs the number of times a heart beats in one minute and the number of years in a lifetime, and then calculates and outputs the number of times it beats in that lifetime.

```
/* program 2.10 - calculates the number of times a heart beats */
/*                in a lifetime.                               */

#include <stdio.h>

unsigned unsignedNumberRead(char prompt[]);
```

```
void main(void)
{
  unsigned beatsPerMinute, years;
  long unsigned beatsInALifetime;

  beatsPerMinute = unsignedNumberRead("Beats per minute? ");
  years = unsignedNumberRead("For how many years? ");
  beatsInALifetime =
               (long unsigned)beatsPerMinute * 60U * 24U *
                                          365.25 * years;
  printf("The number of beats in a lifetime is %lu \n",
                                      beatsInALifetime);
}

unsigned unsignedNumberRead(char prompt[])
{
  char string[BUFSIZ];
  unsigned aNumber = 0u;

  printf("%s", prompt);
  gets(string);
  sscanf(string, "%u", &aNumber);
  return aNumber;
}
```

An example of a program run is

```
Beats per minute? 70
For how many years? 70
The number of beats in a lifetime is 2577204000
```

## 2.8 Documentation

The names chosen for variables should be descriptive; they should reflect the purpose of the object they name. Descriptive variable names help to make programs easier for (human) readers to understand. Variable names should be written in lower case letters and digits, except the first letter in each word which makes up the name; these should be written in upper case. However, the first letter in a variable name should be a lower-case letter.

## 2.9 Programming Principles

- Remember that a variable is a container; it is a location in memory which has a name and which contains a value.

- Choose appropriate types for the values to be used in a calculation.
- Work out each each step of a calculation using pencil and paper (and not a calculator – why?) so that you can check whether your program is giving you the correct answers.
- Take extra care when using values of different types in a calculation.
- Remember that dividing by zero is **never allowed**; ensure that division by zero cannot happen.

*Exercise 2.4*

1 Write a program which will convert a whole number weight in pounds to a weight in kilograms. (One pound weight equals 0.45 kilograms.)

2 Write a program which will input an amount of money (that is, a bill) for goods or services, add value-added tax (VAT) at 17.5% and output the bill including VAT.

3 The maximum mortgage usually allowed on a house is 95% of its value. Write a program which will input the value of a house and output 95% of that value.

4 Write a program which will input hours worked and hourly rate of pay, calculate and output gross pay, tax at 33% of gross pay and net pay.

5 Write a program which will input a whole number of hours and convert it into days and hours, e.g. 27 hours input converts to one day and three hours output.

6 The owner of a restaurant needs a simple program to calculate running costs. The cost of feeding a group of people depends on how many there are (the greater the number of people, the greater the cost of the food they consume) and on the overheads (such as cooks wages, rent and insurance) which have to be paid even if there are no people to feed. The formula is

costOfFeeding = numberOfPeople × costOfFoodPerPerson + overheads

Write a program which will allow the user to enter number of people, the cost of food per person and the overheads, and which will calculate and display the total cost of feeding the group.

7 Write a program which will input an amount of money and output the maximum number of fifty-pound notes that may be contained in the amount of money input. For example, £175 contains at most three fifty-pound notes.

8 Write a program which will input an amount of money and output the money left over when the maximum number of twenty-pound notes have been removed from the amount input. For example, £3 remains after removing four twenty-pound notes from £83.

9 A program is required which will tell a clerk how to make up an employee's pay packet. Fifty-, twenty-, ten- and five-pound notes are to be used together with pound coins. Pence are to be held over and accumulated until they make up over one pound. For example, if an employee's wage is £193.56 then the pay packet would contain three fifty-pound notes, two twenty-pound notes and three one-pound coins; the 56 pence will be added to next week's pay. Write a program which will input an employee's wage as a whole number of pounds,

and output the number of notes of each denomination, together with pound coins, to make up the employee's pay packet.

10 A run-time error occurs during program execution when, for example, an attempt is made to divide by zero or an attempt is made to store a value in a variable which is too small to contain it. Write and run a program which demonstrates a run-time error.

11 A flea weighs about 0.00005 kilograms and, when jumping, exerts a force of about 150 times its own weight in moving its body upwards a distance of about 0.0015 metres before its legs lose contact with the surface on which it was resting. Write a program which will calculate the height jumped according to the formula

$$\text{Height jumped} = \frac{\text{force} \times \text{distance}}{\text{weight} \times 10}$$

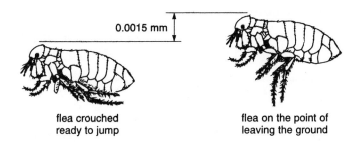

0.0015 mm

flea crouched
ready to jump

flea on the point of
leaving the ground

# 3

## Selections

### 3.1 Boolean Expressions

We can represent whole numbers as points along a line (known as a number line).

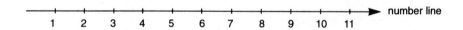

We can see from the number line that, for example, 3 is less than 4 and 4 is more than 3. Is-less-than is represented by the symbol < and is-more-than is represented by >. We write 3 < 4 and 4 > 3.

The expression (3 < 4) has a value; this value is TRUE. Similarly (4 > 3) has the value TRUE.

The expression (4 < 3) has the value FALSE. (How can four be less than three?) Similarly (3 > 4) has the value FALSE.

Expressions which can only have either TRUE or FALSE as their values are known as Boolean expressions.

The symbols < and > are examples of relational operators. In C the relational operators are shown in Figure 3.1.

```
<    is less than
<=   is less than or equal to
>    is more than
>=   is more than or equal to
==   is equal to
!=   is not equal to
```

**Figure 3.1**  The relational operators.

So, for example,

*(4 <= 4)* is TRUE
*(4 == 4)* is TRUE
*(4 != 4)* is FALSE

Notice that, where two symbols are used together, the = symbol is always the last one written, and that there are no spaces between them.

## 3.2   One-way Selection

The purpose of the first program in this chapter is to input a number representing a mark obtained in an examination, and, if that mark is 40 or more, to output the message "Passed.". Here is the program.

```
/* program 3.1 - inputs an exam mark, outputs Pass if the */
/*                mark is 40 or more.                       */

#include <stdio.h>

unsigned unsignedNumberRead(char []);

enum { passMark = 40u };

void main(void)
{
  unsigned mark = unsignedNumberRead("Examination mark?  ");

  if (mark >= passMark)
    printf("Passed.");
  printf("\n");
}

unsigned unsignedNumberRead(char prompt[])
{
  char string[BUFSIZ];
  unsigned aNumber = 0u;

  printf("%s", prompt);
  gets(string);
  sscanf(string, "%u", &aNumber);
  return aNumber;
}
```

Three examples of program runs are

```
(1)   Examination mark? 41
      Passed.

(2)   Examination mark? 40
      Passed.

(3)   Examination mark? 39
```

The line

```
enum { passMark = 40u };
```

defines *passMark* to be the *unsigned* value forty. Since the value of *passMark* cannot be subsequently changed by a program statement, it is an example of a constant. The C keyword *enum* stands for enumeration. An enumeration is just a list of named items, separated by commas, and enclosed within curly brackets or braces. So, *passMark* is an example of an enumerated constant. An enumerated constant is always an integer value.

The Boolean expression

```
(mark >= passMark)
```

is either TRUE (when *mark* is 41 for example) or FALSE (when *mark* is 39 for example). So, the statement

```
if (mark >= passMark)
   printf("Passed.");
```

says that *Passed.* is displayed only if *(mark >= passMark)* is TRUE. If *(mark >= passMark)* is FALSE, then no consequent action is specified. This is why, in example 3 of the program run shown above, no result is shown when the value 39 was entered by the program user.

## 3.3   Two-way Selection

The purpose of the next program is to display *Passed.* if the exam mark entered is 40 or more, but to output *Failed.* if the exam mark is less than 40.

```
/* program 3.2 - inputs an exam mark, outputs Pass     */
/*                if the mark is 40 or more, otherwise  */
/*                outputs Fail.                         */

#include <stdio.h>
```

```
unsigned unsignedNumberRead(char []);
enum { passMark = 40u };

void main(void)
{
  unsigned mark = unsignedNumberRead("Examination mark? ");

  if (mark >= passMark)
    printf("Passed.");
  else
    printf("Failed.");
  printf("\n");
}

unsigned unsignedNumberRead(char prompt[])
{
  char string[BUFSIZ];
  unsigned aNumber = 0u;

  printf("%s", prompt);
  gets(string);
  sscanf(string, "%u", &aNumber);
  return aNumber;
}
```

Three examples of program runs are

(1)   Examination mark? **41**
       Passed.

(2)   Examination mark? **40**
       Passed.

(3)   Examination mark? **39**
       Failed.

If the Boolean expression *(mark >= passMark)* is TRUE then the message *Passed.* is displayed; but if *(mark >= passMark)* is FALSE then *Failed.* is displayed. Either one message or the other is selected for output depending on whether *(mark >= passMark)* is TRUE or FALSE.

```
if (mark >= passMark)
  printf("Passed.");   ← done if (mark >= passMark) is TRUE
else
  printf("Failed.");   ← done if (mark >= passMark) is FALSE
```

Both *if* and *else* are C keywords. *else* cannot be used without a corresponding *if*. Notice that a semi-colon does not follow a Boolean expression such as *(mark >= passMark)*; neither does a semi-colon follow the *else* keyword.

We follow the convention that

- statements written below an if are indented by two spaces
- *else* is written directly in line underneath the *if*
- statements written below an *else* are also indented by two spaces.

Indentation helps us to see logical structure "at a glance".

### Exercise 3.1

1 Write a program which will prompt the user to enter an integer value to represent a person's age, input their response and output whether or not the person is entitled to hold a provisional driving licence. Assume that the minimum age for a provisional licence holder is 17. Your program should use an enumerated constant for the minimum age.
2 To become a member of my millionaires club you have to have about one million pounds, or more, in your bank account. Write a program which will input a number to represent the amount of money in a person's bank account and to output whether that person is eligible for membership of my club.
3 The area of green algae which covers a pond doubles every day. Write a program which will input the area of the pond and the area currently covered by the green algae, and will either output the warning "The pond will be completely covered tomorrow!" if the area currently covered is more than half of the area of the pond, or output the reassuring message "Nothing to worry about!" if otherwise. Use integer values to represent the area of the pond and green algae.

## 3.4   Multi-way Selection

Grades are awarded to students depending on the percentage mark they obtain in a test. Students who obtain 60% or more gain a Merit. Students who obtain between 40% and 59% gain a Pass. Students who obtain less than 40% are graded Refer. The purpose of the next program is to input an integer value to represent a percentage mark and to output the corresponding grade: Merit, Pass, or Refer.

```
/* program 3.3 - inputs a percentage mark, outputs the */
/*               corresponding grade.                   */

#include <stdio.h>

unsigned unsignedNumberRead(char []);
```

```
enum { passMark = 40u, meritMark = 60u };

void main(void)
{
  unsigned mark = unsignedNumberRead("Examination mark? ");

  if (mark >= meritMark)
    printf("Merit.");
  else if (mark >= passMark)
    printf("Passed.");
  else
    printf("Failed.");
  printf("\n");
}

unsigned unsignedNumberRead(char prompt[])
{
  char string[BUFSIZ];
  unsigned aNumber = 0u;

  printf("%s", prompt);
  gets(string);
  sscanf(string, "%u", &aNumber);
  return aNumber;
}
```

Let us examine the program to see what happens for various values of *mark*.

Suppose *mark* has the value 65. Then *(mark >= meritMark)* is TRUE and *Merit.* is displayed.

Suppose now *mark* has the value 50. Then *(mark >= meritMark)* is FALSE but *(mark >= passMark)* is TRUE. So, *Pass.* is displayed.

And again, suppose *mark* now has the value 30. Then, *(mark >= meritMark)* is FALSE and *(mark >= passMark)* is FALSE. Therefore, *Refer.* is displayed.

The table shown in Figure 3.2 illustrates the point.

| case | mark | (mark >= meritMark)? | (mark <= passMark)? | Outcome |
|---|---|---|---|---|
| 1 | 65 | TRUE | not tested | Merit |
| 2 | 50 | FALSE | TRUE | Pass |
| 3 | 30 | FALSE | FALSE | Refer |

**Figure 3.2** If the mark is 65, then the first Boolean expression (mark >= meritMark) is TRUE and consequently no other Boolean expression is evaluated. If the mark is 50 then the first Boolean expression is FALSE but the second Boolean expression (mark >= passMark) is TRUE and consequently Pass is displayed. if the mark is 30, then none of the Boolean expressions are TRUE and Refer is displayed.

So, understanding a sequence of else–if's is easy: look down the sequence of Boolean expressions, in the order written, and stop at the first one which is TRUE, then do the consequent action(s), and then skip to the end of the *if ... else if ... else ...* construction; if none of the Boolean expressions is TRUE, then do the actions following the *else* (if any).

## 3.5  Boundary Testing

Let us look again at the selection statement in program 3.3.

```
if (mark >= meritMark)
   printf("Merit");
else if (mark >= passMark)
   printf("Passed.");
else
   printf("Failed.");
printf("\n");
```

Take the first Boolean expression *(mark >= meritMark)*. We know that *meritMark ==* *60*. *meritMark* represents a boundary value because if mark is just over 60, then *Merit.* would be displayed, but if *mark* is just under 60, then *Pass.* would be displayed.

And again. Take the second Boolean expression *(mark >= passMark)*. We know that *passMark == 40*. If *mark* is just over 40, then *Pass.* would be displayed; if *mark* is just under 40, then *Refer.* would be displayed. *passMark* is an example of a boundary value.

A boundary occurs whenever a small change in the value of a variable causes a large change in the behaviour of a program. For example, the small change in *mark* from 39 to 40 causes the message to be displayed to be changed from *Refer.* to *Pass.*

The purpose of testing a program is to locate errors. A useful strategy is to choose data values just under, just on and just over each boundary (because experience has shown that errors sometimes occur around these points). The data values chosen to test a program are documented in a test plan. A test plan is shown in Figure 3.3 opposite.

This test plan shows that program 3.3 is to be tested 6 times. In the first test, the value input to *mark* is going to be 61 because that is just over the *meritMark* boundary; the anticipated result is that *Merit.* is going to be displayed on the screen. And similarly for tests 2, 3, 4, 5 and 6. Knowing what results to expect is essential, because, otherwise, how would you know whether your program is working correctly?

## 3.6  Test Logs

A test plan outlines your intentions for testing a program. A test log records what actually happened when you tested your program according to your test plan. An example of a test log is shown in Figure 3.4.

**TEST PLAN**

| **Author** | Terry Marris | **Date** | 13 February 1994 |
|---|---|---|---|

**Program** program 3.3

| Test Number | Test Data | Reason | Expected Result |
|---|---|---|---|
| 1 | mark = 61 | just over meritMark | Merit. shown |
| 2 | 60 | just on meritMark | Merit. shown |
| 3 | 59 | just under meritMark | Pass. shown |
| 4 | mark = 41 | just over passMark | Pass. shown |
| 5 | 40 | just on passMark | Pass shown |
| 6 | 39 | just under passMark | Refer. shown |

**Figure 3.3**   Test plan for program 3.3.

**TEST LOG**

| **Author** | Terry Marris | **Date** | 13 February 1994 |
|---|---|---|---|

**Program** program 3.3

| Date | Time | Test Number | Actual Result |
|---|---|---|---|
| Feb 13 | 10.30 | 1 | Merit displayed |
| | | 2 | Merit displayed |
| | | 3 | Pass displayed |
| | | 4 | Pass displayed |
| | | 5 | Pass displayed |
| | | 6 | Refer displayed |

**Figure 3.4**   Test log obtained when running program 3.3.

The test numbers correspond to the test numbers used in the test plan for program 3.3.

A test log is a factual, truthful, honest, historical account of your program testing, errors and all! If your actual results do not match the expected results, then a mistake has been made somewhere. If you discover a mistake then you either document it (by discussing it in a report or mentioning it where it can be seen) or you correct it. It is far better to acknowledge errors in your program than to pretend they never occurred.

### Exercise 3.2

1 Explain, with the aid of examples, the difference between the two C operators = and ==.
2 Amend program 3.3 so that if a mark greater than 100 or less than 0 is entered, the message "Invalid mark – mark should be between 0 and 100 inclusive." is displayed. Construct a test plan for the program then test your program according to your test plan. Correct your program if necessary. Do not forget to complete a test log as you test your program.

### 3.7   Boolean Variables and Logical Operators

The Right One is a dating agency which attempts to introduce each client to a compatible partner of the opposite sex. One particular client is looking for a partner who is between the ages of 25 and 30 inclusive. The purpose of the next program is to input a potential partner's age details and to output whether they match the age requirements.

```
/* program 3.4 - decides whether a person would make a */
/*               suitable partner on the basis of age. */

#include <stdio.h>

unsigned unsignedNumberRead(char []);

enum { minimumAge = 25u, maximumAge = 30u };


void main(void)
{
  unsigned age = unsignedNumberRead("How old are you? ");
  int ageIsOK = (age >= minimumAge) && (age <= maximumAge);

  if (ageIsOK)
    printf("You will do!");
  else
    printf("Sorry - I am not interested.");
  printf("\n");
}
```

```
unsigned unsignedNumberRead(char prompt[])
{
    char string[BUFSIZ];
    unsigned aNumber = 0u;

    printf("%s", prompt);
    gets(string);
    sscanf(string, "%u", &aNumber);
    return aNumber;
}
```

Examples of program runs are:

```
(1)    How old are you? 24
       Sorry - I am not interested.
```

```
(2)    How old are you? 25
       You will do!
```

```
(3)    How old are you? 26
       You will do!
```

```
(4)    How old are you? 29
       You will do!
```

```
(5)    How old are you? 30
       You will do!
```

```
(6)    How old are you? 31
       Sorry - I am not interested.
```

Let us examine the statement

```
int ageIsOK = (age >= minimumAge) && (age <= maximumAge);
```

Working from right to left: *(age <= maximumAge)* is a Boolean expression with value either TRUE or FALSE. *(age >= minimumAge)* is also a Boolean expression. The double ampersand, *&&*, means and-at-the-same-time. So, the whole expression

```
(age >= minimumAge) && (age <= maximumAge)
```

which says that *age* is greater than (or equal to) *minimumAge* and-at-the-same-time *age* is less than (or equal to) *maximumAge*, is also a Boolean expression with value either TRUE or FALSE.

In C, TRUE is represented by a non-zero value, usually one; FALSE is represented by zero. So we can assign the value of the Boolean expression *(age >= minimumAge) && (age <= maximumAge)* to a variable of type *int*. This is what we have done here:

```
int ageIsOK = (age >= minimumAge) && (age <= maximumAge);
```

Then we can go on to write

```
if (ageIsOK)
  printf("You will do!");
else
  printf("Sorry - I am not interested.");
```

where the statement is read as *if ageIsOK is TRUE then printf "You will do" otherwise printf "Sorry - I am not interested." ageIsOK* is a Boolean expression with value either TRUE (that is, one) or FALSE (that is, zero).

We follow the convention that variables intended to represent Boolean values include the word *is* in their name. So, for example, *ageIsOK* is either TRUE, or it is not.

Returning to the Right One Dating Agency, another client is looking for a partner who is either rich or good looking; their ideal partner is either rich or is good-looking (or both rich and good-looking). The purpose of the next program is to input a potential partner's financial situation and appearance, and to output whether they meet the requirements for a suitable partner.

```
/* program 3.5 - decides whether a person would make a   */
/*               suitable partner on the basis of money  */
/*               and looks.                               */
#include <stdio.h>


void main(void)
{
  int isRich;
  int isGoodLooking;
  char reply[BUFSIZ];

  printf("Are you rich? ");
  gets(reply);
  isRich = (reply[0] == 'y') || (reply[0] == 'Y');

  printf("Are you good looking? ");
  gets(reply);
  isGoodLooking = (reply[0] == 'y') || (reply[0] == 'Y');
```

```
  if ((isRich) || (isGoodLooking))
    printf("You will do!");
  else
    printf("Sorry - I am not interested.");
}
```

Some examples of program runs are

(1)    Are you rich? **y**
       Are you good looking? **y**
       You will do!

(2)    Are you rich? **Y**
       Are you good looking? **n**
       You will do!

(3)    Are you rich? **n**
       Are you good looking? **Y**
       You will do!

(4)    Are you rich? **N**
       Are you good looking? **N**
       Sorry - I am not interested.

The lines

```
  if ((isRich) || (isGoodLooking))
    printf("You will do!");
  else
    printf("Sorry - I am not interested.");
```

say that if either *isRich* is TRUE OR *isGoodLooking* is TRUE (or both *isRich* and *isGoodLooking* are TRUE) then print *You will do*, otherwise, if neither *isRich* nor *IsGoodLooking* are TRUE, then print *Sorry - I am not interested*.

The expression *reply[0]* refers to the first character stored in *reply*. The statement

```
  isRich = (reply[0] == 'y') || (reply[0] == 'Y');
```

says "store TRUE in *isRich* if the first character stored in *reply* is either y or Y, otherwise store FALSE in *isRich*". || means 'or'.

## 3.8 Documentation

Statements sandwiched between *if* and *else* are to be indented by two character spaces to help the human reader understand the structure at a glance. *else* is to be written in line directly below the *if*. If a statement sequence comprises several statements, then the braces should be positioned as shown below:

```
if (boolean-expression) {
  statement;
  statement;
    ...
}
else {
  statement;
  statement;
  statement;
    ...
}
```

For example

```
if (currentTransaction > availableCredit) {
  printf("Credit limit exceeded - transaction refused.\n");
  printf("Inform customer.\n");
}
else {
  printf("Proceed with transaction.\n");
  printf("Check signature.\n");
}
```

Test Plans – see Figure 3.2 – are used to design and specify data values to test programs in a systematic manner. They are used to record items such as data values intended to show that the program works according to its specification, reasons for using particular test data values and the expected results of running the program with the test data.

Test Logs – see Figure 3.3 – are used to record the results of actually running programs with the test data. If the results actually obtained do not match the expected results, then a mistake has been made somewhere. Test logs must be written by hand at the time of testing and should include details such as test run number, time, date and actual result.

## 3.9 Programming Principles

Use enumerated constants and Boolean expressions wherever their use makes the program logic clearer to the human reader.

Remember that program users might input characters in either lower or upper case; they should be allowed to do so. It is up to the programmer to take appropriate action.

With a sequence of *else if*'s arrange the Boolean expressions in the correct order to obtain the desired results.

*Exercise 3.3*

**Remember to include test plan and test logs with every program you write.**

1 An important principle is "if it is working, then do not fix it!". Write and test a C program which will ask the user whether their program is working correctly, and to output appropriate advice.

2 The Right One is a dating agency which attempts to introduce each client to a compatible partner. One particular client is looking for a partner who is a non-smoker and who does not eat meat. Design, write and test a program which will input a potential partner's smoking and eating habits and output whether the person would make a suitable partner.

3 A television rental company will rent a TV to a customer if the customer is not on the bankrupt list **and** the customer's name and address appear in the register of eligible voters **and** the customer is currently employed **and** has been in full-time employment for the past two years.

   Write a program which will ask the user to reply to questions such as "Is customer on the bankrupt list (y/n)?", "Is customer on the electoral roll (y/n)?", "Is the customer currently employed (y/n)" and output whether a TV should be rented to the customer or not.

4 Design, write and test a program to the following specification. The program is to be a model for processing credit card transactions. Inputs: credit limit, credit used, bill for goods or services. Outputs: "OK" if credit used + bill is not greater than credit limit, otherwise "Transaction refused".

5 A year is a leap year if it is divisible by 4 but not by 100 except that years divisible by 400 are leap years. So, for example, 1992 is a leap year (divisible by 4); but 1900 is not a leap year (divisible by 4 and divisible by 100); but 2000 is a leap year (divisible by 400). Design, write and test a program which will display "Is a leap year" or "Is not a leap year" depending on the value of an integer input to represent a year. Hint: a number is divisible by 4 if the remainder after division by 4 is 0.

6 Electricity meter readings are five-digit numbers. If a meter reaches 99999, then it restarts at 00000. Every three months the meter is read. The number of electricity units used in the previous three months is calculated from the present and previous meter readings. Usually, the previous meter reading is less than the present meter reading; however, when the meter reaches 99999 and restarts at 00000, the previous meter reading could be greater than the present meter reading. Design, write and test a program which will input the present and previous meter readings and output the number of units used together with the cost of the electricity used if the charge per unit is £0.08 and the standing charge is £9.50. (The standing charge is payable irrespective of the amount of electricity used.)

# 4

## Functions

### 4.1 Introduction

We have already used library functions such as *printf*, *gets* and *sscanf* in our programs. We have used our own functions – *unsignedNumberRead*, *intNumberRead* and *doubleNumberRead* for example. In this chapter we will design and write some functions for ourselves. We start with a simple example.

### 4.2 Designing and Implementing Functions

Let us suppose that a function which adds two *int* numbers together and gives us the result is useful. The result supplied by the function is the sum of two *int* numbers. So we name the function *intSum*. The function requires two *int* values to add together; these are to be supplied to the function from another source. (We are not concerned with where the values come from, only with what to do with them once we have them.) We shall name these two values $X$ and $Y$. Now we can write the function prototype thus

```
int intSum(int X, int Y);
```

Reading from right to left, this function prototype tells us that the function requires two *int* values – named $X$ and $Y$ here, that its name is *intSum*, and that its result is an *int* value.

The items enclosed within brackets and separated by a comma, namely *int X* and *int Y*, are known as parameters.

We have to place some restrictions on the parameters. First, both $X$ and $Y$ must contain *int* values. Second, we cannot allow the value of *X plus Y* to be too large to fit into an *int* variable. We express these restrictions as pre-conditions thus

```
int intSum(int X, int Y);
/* pre-condition: X + Y <= INT_MAX */
```

The pre-condition *X and Y must both contain int values* is implied by the parameters defined in the function prototype. And so they do need to be explicitly mentioned.

If the values supplied meet the restrictions, then we will guarantee that the function will supply the correct result. We express this in a post-condition thus

```
int intSum(int X, int Y);
/* pre-condition: X + Y <= INT_MAX */
/* post-condition: returns X + Y    */
```

Pre-conditions describe what must be true on entry to a function if the function is to perform as required. Post-conditions describe what must be true on exit from a function when the function has completed its task. A function prototype, together with a set of pre- and post-conditions, is known as a function specification.

Given a function's specification, we can use it without knowing or even caring how the function actually works. For example

```
(a)    int sumOfInts = intSum(2, 3);

(b)    int jockeysWeight = 96;
       int saddleWeight = 7;
       int sumOfWeights = intSum(jockeysWeight, saddleWeight);
```

When the function is used as in

```
int sumOfInts = intSum(2, 3);
```

the value *2* is passed to *X* and the value *3* is passed to *Y*. The values *2* and *3* are examples of argument values. The order in which the arguments are written must match the order in which the parameters are written. So, when the function starts to perform its task, *X* contains *2* and *Y* contains *3*. When the function completes its task, the function result, 5 in this example, is stored in *sumOfInts*. We say that a function returns a value. The value returned may be assigned to a variable (as in this example) or used in an expression (as we shall see).

When the function is used, as in

```
int jockeysWeight = 96;
int saddleWeight = 7;
int sumOfWeights = intSum(jockeysWeight, saddleWeight);
```

a copy of the value stored in *jockeysWeight* (namely *96*) is passed to *X* and a copy of the value stored in *saddleWeight* (namely *7*) is passed to *Y*. Figure 4.1 on the next page illustrates the point.

When the function *intSum* begins to perform its task, *X* contains *96* and *Y* contains *7*. When the function completes its task, the value returned by the function, namely 96 + 7 == 103, is stored in *sumOfWeights*.

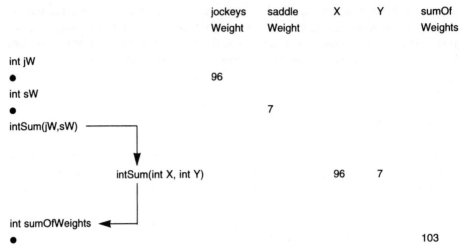

**Figure 4.1**  Initially, jockeysWeight (jW) contains 96 and saddleWeight (sW) contains 7. Then a call to intSum is made. X receives a copy of jockeysWeight contents and Y receives a copy of saddleWeight contents; consequently, X contains 96 and Y contains 7. Then intSum returns its result and 103 is placed in sumofWeights.

Argument and parameter names need not be the same, but the order in which they are written must match each other. Consequently, a single function may be used in many different contexts.

Let us see how the function *intSum* actually works; its implementation is straight-forward.

```
int intSum(int X, int Y)
{
   return X + Y;
}
```

The C keyword *return* returns you to the point where the function was called, and, in this case, the value of $X + Y$ is sent there also. Let us see how the function would be used in a complete program.

```
/* program 4.1 - uses intSum function. */


#include <stdio.h>


int intNumberRead(char prompt[]);
/* post-condition: returns int value from the keyboard.    */
```

```
int intSum(int X, int Y);                    ← function prototype with
/* pre-condition: X + Y <= INT_MAX */          two int parameters
/* post-condition: returns X + Y     */


void main(void)
{
   int a = intNumberRead("Number? ");
   int b = intNumberRead("Another number? ");
   int c = intSum(a, b);                     ← function call with
                                               arguments a and b.
   printf("Their sum is %d\n", c);
}

int intNumberRead(char prompt[])
{
   char string[BUFSIZ];
   int number = 0;

   printf("%s", prompt);
   gets(string);
   sscanf(string, "%d", &number);
   return number;
}

int intSum(int X, int Y)                     ← function heading with
{                                              parameters X and Y
   return X + Y;
}
```

An example of a program run is

```
Number? 3
Another number 2
Their sum is 5
```

A function implementation is known in C as a function definition. The functions which make up the program may be written in any order. But we follow the convention that *main* is the first function written, and that the other functions are written in alphabetical order. A function prototype must come before its implementation and call.

In general, a function takes some argument values, stores them in parameter variables, performs some task on the parameter values and returns a single value as its result. The values that may be returned by a function include those of type *char*, *int* and *double*. Let us look at another simple example.

Value-added tax (VAT) is charged at different rates for different goods or services. Let us write a simple function which will receive two argument values – one representing the cost of some goods or services and one representing the rate of VAT to be charged. The function is to return the total cost of the goods. We shall name the function *costPlusVat*. Here is the function specification.

```
double costPlusVat(double cost, double vatRate);
/* pre-condition: cost + cost * vatRate < DBL_MAX     */
/* post-condition: returns cost with VAT added to it. */
```

Given the following variable definitions and assignments

```
double cost = 100.00;
double generalVatRate = 0.175;   /* 17.5% */
```

the function may be used like this

```
double costWithVat = costPlusVat(cost, generalVatRate);
```

The argument values, *100.00* and *0.175*, are passed to, and stored in, the function parameter variables *cost* and *vatRate*. The function adds VAT to the *cost* and returns the total cost, which is then stored in the variable *costWithVat*.

The implementation of *costPlusVat* is straightforward

```
double costPlusVat(double cost, double vatRate)
{
   return cost + cost * vatRate;
}
```

And a final example: students are graded on their exam performance as either satisfactory if they obtain 40% or more, and unsatisfactory otherwise. We shall write a function which receives, as its argument value, an integer to represent a percentage mark, and which returns 'u' if the mark is less than 40 or 's' if the mark is 40 or more. We shall not place any special restrictions on the argument value except that it should not be negative. We shall name the function *gradeFromMark*. Here is its specification.

```
char gradeFromMark(unsigned mark);
/* post-condition: returns 'u' if mark < 40, otherwise
returns 's'. */
```

An example of its use is

```
mark = 50u;
char grade = gradeFromMark(mark);
```

```
if (grade == 'u')
   printf("Include student on unsatisfactory list.\n");
else if (grade == 's')
   printf("Include student on satisfactory list.\n");
```

In C, *char* constant values are written within single quotation marks. So the character constants *u* and *s* are written in C as '*u*' and '*s*'.

An implementation for *gradeFromMark* is

```
char gradeFromMark(unsigned mark)
{
   if (mark < 40u)
      return 'u';
   else
      return 's';
}
```

The problem with using *u* to represent unsatisfactory is that we have to remember what *u* means. It would be better to use a more descriptive term such as the word *unsatisfactory* itself.

C allows us to define our own constant enumerated values (see program 3.1 for example). We shall extend this to define our own type named *Grade*.

```
typedef enum { unsatisfactory, satisfactory } Grade;
```

*typedef* is a C keyword. It is used to provide an alternative name for an existing data type. Here, we have given the name *Grade* to the *enum* data type {*unsatisfactory, satisfactory*}. Having defined a data type we can define variables of this type.

```
Grade grade;
```

And we can declare functions to return a value of this type.

```
Grade gradeFromMark(unsigned mark);
```

Here, we have followed the convention that type names chosen by ourselves begin with an upper-case letter. (Variable and function names always begin with a lower-case letter so we can see at a glance which is a type and which is a variable or function.)

We enhance the specification by writing

```
Grade gradeFromMark(unsigned mark);
/* post-condition: returns unsatisfactory if mark < 39, */
/*                 otherwise returns satisfactory.      */
```

Program 4.2 shown below displays either *Place student on unsatisfactory list* or *Place student on satisfactory list* depending on the value returned by the *gradeFromMark* function.

```
/* program 4.2 - grades a student as either satisfactory */
/*                or unsatisfactory.                      */

#include <stdio.h>

typedef enum { unsatisfactory, satisfactory } Grade;


Grade gradeFromMark(unsigned mark);
/* post-condition: returns unsatisfactory if mark < 40, */
/*                 otherwise returns satisfactory.      */

unsigned unsignedNumberRead(char prompt[]);
/* post-condition: returns number entered at the keyboard. */

void main(void)
{
  Grade grade;
  unsigned mark = unsignedNumberRead("Student's mark? ");

  grade = gradeFromMark(mark);
  if (grade == unsatisfactory)
    printf("Place student on unsatisfactory list.\n");
  else
    printf("Place student on satisfactory list.\n");
}

Grade gradeFromMark(unsigned mark)
{
  if (mark < 40)
    return unsatisfactory;
  else
    return satisfactory;
}

unsigned unsignedNumberRead(char prompt[])
{
  char string[BUFSIZ];
  unsigned number = 0u;
```

```
    printf("%s", prompt);
    gets(string);
    sscanf(string, "%u", &number);
    return number;
}
```

Two examples of program runs are

(1)   Student's mark? **39**
      Place student on unsatisfactory list.

(2)   Student's mark? **40**
      Place student on satisfactory list.

*Exercise 4.1*

**1** A building society will lend up to about three times the annual salary of a person applying for a mortgage. Design, write and test a function which will take two argument values – a salary and a multiplier – and return the maximum loan allowed on that salary.

**2** The cost of materials used in manufacturing a simple double-glazed, non-opening rectangular window depends on its size. Design, write and test a function which will take four argument values – the length and height in metres of a window, the cost of the frame material per metre and the cost of the glass per square metre, and which will return the total cost of the materials.

**3** Competitors in a marathon are categorised, according to their age, as either junior, regular or senior. Design, write and test a function which will receive, as an argument value, a competitor's age and return junior if age is less than 17, regular if age is between 17 and 39 inclusive and senior if age is 40 or more.

**4** Write a function which will calculate and return the car parking charge payable if the charge is £0.75 per hour (or part hour). Your function should have three parameters – the arrival and departure times in 24-hour clock notation, and the unit charge.

## 4.3 Some Useful Functions

We often need to ask a program user a question which invites a yes or no answer. For example: Married (y/n)? Are you currently employed (y/n)? Aged over 40 (y/n)? Let us design and write a function to do the task. First, we name the function *yesOrNo* since we require the function result to represent either *yes* or *no* (or *TRUE* or *FALSE*). The function parameter – only one in this case – is going to be text, that is, a string literal. So the parameter is a sequence of char. We do not need to place any special restrictions on the argument value. Now we can write the function specification.

```
int yesOrNo(char prompt[]);
/* post-condition: returns either 0 for FALSE or No,      */
/*                      1 for TRUE or Yes.                 */
```

An example of its use is

```
int hasAGrant;
int isAFullTimeStudent = yesOrNo(
                "Are you a full time student (y/n)? ");

if (isAFullTimeStudent)
  hasAGrant = yesOrNo("Do you have a grant (y/n)? ");

if ((isAFullTimeStudent) && (hasAGrant))
  printf("Loan application accepted.\n");
else
  printf("Loan application rejected.\n");
```

Let us see how the function may be implemented.

```
int yesOrNo(char prompt[])
{
  char string[BUFSIZ];

  prints("%s", prompt);
  gets(string);
  return (string[0] == 'y') || (string[0] == 'Y') ||
         (string[0] == 't') || (string[0] == 'T');
}
```

*string* is a variable which can store a sequence of up to *BUFSIZ* (*BUFSIZ*, defined in *stdio.h*, is usually *255*) characters. The place where each character is stored in string is identified by a number. The first storage location is always numbered zero. So the string literal *Yes* would be stored in the variable *string* like this

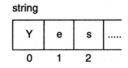

We are only interested in the first character stored. We identify the first character stored in *string* by writing *string[0]*. In our example here, *string[0]* contains the *char Y*. In C, *char* constant values are enclosed within single quotes. So we can write

```
string[0] == 'Y'
```

The statement

```
return (string[0] == 'y') || (string[0] == 'Y') ||
       (string[0] == 't') || (string[0] == 'T');
```

says return TRUE (that is, one) if the first character stored in *string* is either 'y' or 'Y' or 't' or 'T', otherwise, return FALSE (that is, zero).

The *yesOrNo* function is used in the following program.

```
/* program 4.3 - uses the yesOrNo function. */

#include <stdio.h>

int yesOrNo(char prompt[]);
/* post-condition: returns either 0 for FALSE or No,   */
/*                 1 for TRUE or Yes.                   */

void main(void)
{
   int canFindError = yesOrNo(
                          "Can you find your error (y/n)? ");

   if (canFindError)
     printf("Then fix it!\n");
   else
     printf("Perhaps you are looking in the wrong place.\n");
}

int yesOrNo(char prompt[])
{
   char string[BUFSIZ];

   printf("%s", prompt);
   gets(string);
   return (string[0] == 'y') || (string[0] == 'Y') ||
          (string[0] == 't') || (string[0] == 'T');
}
```

Two examples of program runs are

```
(1)   Can you find your error (y/n)? y
      Then fix it.

(2)   Can you find your error (y/n)? N
      Then perhaps you are looking in the wrong place.
```

Now we consider another example. Deciding whether two *double* values are equal or not is a bit of a problem. For example, in some circumstances we might agree that 3.999 is the same as 4.000. And in some circumstances we might agree that these two values are not the same. To complicate matters a little more, we cannot guarantee that values of type *double* (or *float*) are stored exactly (because they are converted into binary format before they are stored in memory, and for some *double* values there is no exact binary equivalent). In all circumstances we shall agree that two *double* values are the same provided they differ by no more than an agreed amount (known as the tolerance). So, if the tolerance is 0.01, then 3.999 would be the same as 4.000 because 4.000 − 3.999 < 0.01. (0.001 is less than 0.01.) However, if the tolerance is 0.0005 then 4.000 would not be the same as 3.999 because 4.000 − 3.999 ≮ 0.0005. (≮ means is-not-less-than.) We shall name the function *doubleEqual*. The function shall have two *double* parameters to represent the two values to be compared, and a third *double* parameter to represent the tolerance. We shall place no special restriction on the argument values except that they be values of type *double*. The function will return an *int* result to represent either TRUE or FALSE. Here is its specification.

```
int doubleEqual(double X, double Y, double tolerance);
/* post-condition: returns 1 if absolute(X - Y) <= tolerance */
/*                 otherwise returns 0.                       */
```

What is this *absolute(X − Y)*? It is the difference between the two values $X$ and $Y$; this difference is always positive (or zero) irrespective of whether $X$ is greater than $Y$, or $Y$ is greater than $X$. So

```
doubleEqual(3.999, 4.000, 0.01) == TRUE;       and
doubleEqual(4.000, 3.999, 0.01) == TRUE;
```

Another example of a call to *doubleEqual* is

```
double actualBallBearingSize = 3.906;
double requiredBallBearingSize = 3.900;
double tolerance = 0.005;

if doubleEqual(actualBallBearingSize,
                    requiredBallBearingSize, tolerance)
   printf("Accept.\n");
else
   printf("Reject.\n");
```

The implementation of *doubleEqual* is straightforward.

```
int doubleEqual(double X, double Y, double tolerance)
{
   return fabs(X - Y) <= tolerance;
}
```

*fabs* returns the absolute double value of its *double* argument. So, for example, *fabs(–0.03)* == *0.03* and *fabs(0.03)* == *0.03*. *fabs* is defined in the *math* library. The function *doubleEqual* returns TRUE (that is, one) if the value returned by *fabs* is less than or equal to *tolerance*, otherwise, *doubleEqual* returns FALSE (that is, zero).

The following program, program 4.4, uses *doubleEqual* to determine whether the amount of money in a supermarket check-out till is close enough to what should be in the till.

```c
/* program 4.4 - uses doubleEqual. */

#include <stdio.h>
#include <math.h>

int doubleEqual(double X, double Y, double tolerance);
/* post-condition: returns 1 if absolute(X - Y) <= tolerance */
/*                 otherwise returns 0.                       */


double doubleNumberRead(char prompt[]);
/* post-condition: returns number entered by the user  */
/*                 at the keyboard. */

void main(void)

{
   double actualMoneyInTill =
          doubleNumberRead("Money actually in till is £");
   double calculatedMoneyInTill =
          doubleNumberRead("Money in till should be £");
   double tolerance = 0.50;

   if (doubleEqual(actualMoneyInTill,
                        calculatedMoneyInTill, tolerance))
     printf("OK\n");
   else
     printf("Money in till does not match expected amount.\n");
}


int doubleEqual(double X, double Y, double tolerance)

{
   return fabs(X - Y) <= tolerance;
}
```

```
double doubleNumberRead(char prompt[])
{
   char string[BUFSIZ];
   double number = 0.0;

   printf("%s", prompt);
   gets(string);
   sscanf(string, "%lf", &number);
   return number;
}
```

Two examples of program runs are

(1)   Money actually in till is **£100.00**
      Money in till should be £99.50
      OK

(2)   Money actually in till is **£100.00**
      Money in till should be £99.49
      Money in till does not match expected amount.

### 4.4   Addresses Passed as Arguments to Function Parameters

Up until now, argument values have been passed strictly in one direction – from the point where the function was called to the function parameters; a function could only return a single value such as an *int*, *char* or *enum* value to its caller. In this section we see how a C function can return several values back to its caller.

We have already written several general-purpose functions such as *intNumberRead* and *doubleNumberRead*. What we need is a function which will read, from the keyboard, a sequence of characters such as somebody's name, and store it in an appropriate variable. An appropriate variable definition would be

```
char personsName[BUFSIZ];
```

Here, the variable identifier is *personsName* and the variable is of type *array of char*. An array is just a named, continuous sequence of numbered storage locations (see Figure 4.2).

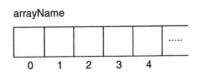

**Figure 4.2**   An array is a named sequence of numbered storage locations.

Each storage location in an array of *char* can hold a single *char* value. In C, a sequence of characters stored in an array of *char* is known as a string. So, a person's name, stored in memory, is an example of a string.

Given the variable definition

```
char personsName[BUFSIZ];
```

a function call to input a string value from the keyboard and store it in *personsName* might be

```
readString("Name? ", personsName);
```

Here is the function's specification.

```
void readString(char prompt[], char string[]);
/* Displays prompt on the screen, inputs string from keyboard.*/
/* post-condition: string' contains characters entered by the */
/*                 user at the keyboard.                       */
```

The square brackets *[ ]* declares the parameter to be an array type. In making the function call, *Name?* is passed to *prompt* and the array *personsName* is passed to *string*. Passing arrays as argument values is a special case in C because, what is actually passed is the address at which the array is located (rather than a copy of the value of a variable, as has been the case up until now). Therefore, in this example, *personsName* and *string* both refer to the same location in memory. The value stored in this array is known as *personsName* in the function call, and as *string* inside the function itself.

The implementation of *readString* is straightforward.

```
void readString(char prompt[], char string[])
{
   printf("%s", prompt);
   gets(string);
}
```

Here is a simple program which uses *readString*.

```
/* program 4.5 - inputs a string, then displays it. */
#include <stdio.h>


void readString(char prompt[], char string[]);
/* post-condition: string' contains character sequence */
/*                 entered by the user at the keyboard. */
```

```
void main(void)
{
  char name[BUFSIZ];

  readString("What is your name? ", name);
  printf("Name entered is %s.\n", name);
}


void readString(char prompt[], char string[])
{
  printf("%s", prompt);
  gets(string);
}
```

An example of a program run is

```
What is your name? Tom Jones
Name entered is Tom Jones.
```

Now let us look at another example. Suppose we need a function which will obtain some personal details such as name, gender and age from the keyboard. Given the following type and variable definitions

```
typedef enum { male, female } Gender;

char name[BUFSIZ];
Gender gender;
unsigned age;
```

an appropriate function call might be

```
getDetails(name, &gender, &age);
```

This time we have to explicitly pass the address of both *gender* and *age* as argument values because neither *gender* nor *age* are arrays. We do this by prefixing the variable name with the & symbol. The & symbol is known as the address operator. Let us look at the corresponding function specification.

```
void getDetails(char name[], Gender *pGender, unsigned *pAge);
  /* pre-condition: pGender contains the address of a      */
  /*                Gender variable,                       */
  /*                pAge contains the address of an        */
  /*                unsigned variable.                     */
```

```
/*  post-condition:name' contains a sequence of         */
/*                     characters,                       */
/*                     *pGender' contains either male or */
/*                     female,                            */
/*                     *pAge' contains an unsigned int value.*/
```

If an address is passed as an argument value, then the corresponding parameter must be capable of storing that address. The parameter declaration is made by prefixing the parameter name with an asterisk, as in *double \*pAge* for example. A variable which stores an address is known as a pointer. So we follow the convention that variables which store addresses have their name prefixed with the letter *p*.

The **\*** used in a variable declaration indicates that the variable is a pointer; it is known in this context as the pointer punctuator.

The **\*** used with a variable refers to the contents of that variable; it is known as the indirection operator. For example, *pGender* contains the address of a location in store (or memory). But *\*pGender* refers to the value stored at that location. We explore the point further as we consider the implementation of *getDetails*.

```
void getDetails(char name[], Gender *pGender, unsigned *pAge)
{
   char string[BUFSIZ];


   readString("Name? ", name);
   *pGender = genderRead("Male or female (m/f)? ");
   *pAge = unsignedNumberRead("Age? ");
}
```

*genderRead* returns either *male* or *female*. Now, *pGender* contains an address of a location in store, that is, a variable. The line

```
   *pGender = genderRead("Male or female (m/f)? ");
```

places either the value *male* or the value *female* into this location.

And again, *pAge* contains the address of a location in store. *\*pAge* refers to the contents of that storage location. So the statement

```
   *pAge = unsignedNumberRead("Age? ");
```

places the value returned by *unsignedNumberRead* into that location. A simple program illustrates the main ideas.

```
/* program 4.6 - uses pointers. */

#include <stdio.h>
```

```
void getAge(unsigned *pAge);
unsigned unsignedNumberRead(char prompt[]);


void main(void)
{
   unsigned age;

   printf("Address of variable age is %u.\n", &age);
   getAge(&age);                              ← address of age
                                                is passed
   printf("Variable age contains %u.\n", age);
}


void getAge(unsigned *pAge)        ← address of age is received in pAge
{
   printf("Parameter pAge contains %u.\n", pAge);
   *pAge = unsignedNumberRead("Person's age? "); ← value at
                                 address contained in pAge is updated
   printf("*pAge contains %u.\n", *pAge);
}


unsigned unsignedNumberRead(char prompt[])
{
   char string[BUFSIZ];
   unsigned number = 0u;

   printf("%s", prompt);
   gets(string);
   sscanf(string, "%u", &number);
   return number;
}
```

An example of a program run is

```
Address of variable age is 65508.
Parameter pAge contains 65508.
Person's age? 26
*pAge contains 26.
age contains 26.
```

In Figure 4.3 we trace the state of the variables at the points marked • in the essential parts of program 4.6.

```
                                          address
       void main(void)                    65508
       {                                   age              pAge
           unsigned age;
       ●                                   ?
           getAge(&age);   void getAge(unsigned *pAge)
                           {
                           ●                                 65508
                               *pAge = unsignedNumberRead("Age? ");
                           ●                  26
                           }
       }
```

**Figure 4.3**   Initially, age, located at address 65508, contains no defined value. The call to getAge is made. Then, pAge contains the address of age, namely 65508. The value returned by unsignedNumberRead, 26, is stored in *pAge, that is, in age.

You may have been wondering about the ' symbol in the post-conditions. A parameter identifier without the prime symbol, ', refers to its value on entry to the function; a parameter identifier with the prime symbol refers to its value on exit from the function. So, the pre-condition

```
pre-condition: pAge contains the address of an unsigned
variable.
```

says that *pAge* is to contain the address of an *unsigned int* variable when the function begins to carry out its task. The post-condition

```
post-condition: *pAge' contains an unsigned int value.
```

says that the variable, whose address is stored in *pAge*, contains an *unsigned int* value immediately the function has completed its task.

## 4.5   Classical Top-down Design

We begin by looking at a simple problem. A program is required which will maintain a person's bank account. The program is to input a transaction, either a withdrawal or a deposit, update the balance in the account and to display the new balance.

We start with a statement of the problem in a single word.

*maintainAccount*

We then add more detail by refining this statement into a sequence of function calls.

*maintainAccount*
　*balance = currentBalance();*
　*transaction = transactionInput();*
　*balance = updatedBalance(transaction, balance);*
　*displayBalance(balance);*

*currentBalance* returns the present balance in the account. *transactionInput* returns the transaction, either withdrawal or deposit, from the keyboard. *updatedBalance* returns the new balance after it has been updated by the transaction. *displayBalance* returns nothing; it merely prints its argument on the screen.

Sometimes, a picture is useful. We describe the structured collection of function calls in a diagram known as a program structure chart (see Figure 4.4).

Now we can easily implement each function as shown in program 4.7.

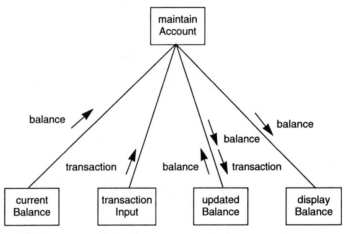

**Figure 4.4** Program structure chart showing that currentBalance returns balance to maintainAccount, transactionInput returns transaction to maintainAccount, updatedBalance receives balance and transaction and returns balance and displayBalance receives balance and returns nothing.

```
/* program 4.7 - maintains a person's bank account. */

#include <stdio.h>


double currentBalance(void);
/* post-condition: returns balance currently in a bank
account. */

void displayBalance(double balance);
```

```
double doubleNumberRead(char prompt[]);
/* post-condition: returns number entered at the keyboard. */


double transactionInput(void);
/* post-condition: returns transaction input at the keyboard. */


double updatedBalance(double transaction, double balance);
/* pre-condition: transaction + balance < DBL_MAX */
/* post-condition: returns transaction + balance  */


void main(void)   /* maintainAccount */
{
   double balance = currentBalance();
   double transaction = transactionInput();

   balance = updatedBalance(transaction, balance);
   displayBalance(balance);
}


double currentBalance(void)
{
   return doubleNumberRead("Current balance £");
}


void displayBalance(double balance)
{
   printf("Current balance is £%0.2f\n", balance);
}


double doubleNumberRead(char prompt[])
{
   char string[BUFSIZ];
   double number = 0.0;

   printf("%s", prompt);
   gets(string);
   sscanf(string, "%lf", &number);
   return number;
}
```

```
double transactionInput(void)
{
   return doubleNumberRead(
              "Transaction (- withdrawal, + deposit) £");
}


double updatedBalance(double transaction, double balance)
{
   return transaction + balance;
}
```

Here is another example. A program is required which will process applications for a marathon race. The program is to input applicants details, put them into categories, assign a competitor number to each person, and to print their details. We shall deal with just one application. We start with a statement of the problem in just one word.

*processApplicant*

We refine this statement by adding more detail in the form of the main function calls required. For each function call, we show its arguments and return value – if any.

*processApplicant*
   *inputApplicants(name, dateOfBirth, gender, age);*
   *category = applicantsCategory(gender, age);*
   *number = competitorNumber();*
   *printCompetitor(name, category, number);*

Then we choose any one of these function calls and expand on it by adding more detail. Let us look at *inputApplicants*.

*inputApplicants(char name[], char dateOfBirth[],*
                                *Gender \*pGender, unsigned \*pAge)*
   *readName(name);*
   *readDate(dateOfBirth);*
   *\*pGender = genderRead();*
   *\*pAge = ageRead();*

We draw the structure chart accordingly as shown in Figure 4.5.
   We repeat this process of refining one function at a time until each function can be easily implemented.
   The essence of the classical top-down design method is

• start with a one-word statement of the problem
• refine the statement into a sequence of function calls

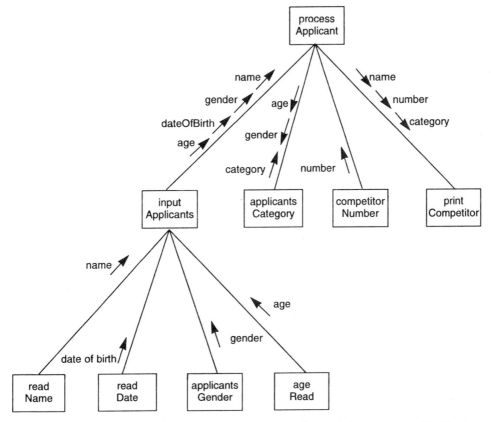

**Figure 4.5** ProcessApplicant calls inputApplicants, applicantsCategory, competitorNumber and printCompetitor. inputApplicants calls readName, readDate, applicantsGender and applicantsNumber.

- consider refining each of these functions into another sequence of calls
- repeat the refine-a-function process until each function can be easily implemented

Classical top-down design results in a program structured as a logical hierarchy of functions.

## 4.6 Documentation

Program structure charts show the hierarchy of function calls and the data items passed between them; see Figures 4.4 and 4.5 for example. You can have several levels of function calls as shown in Figure 4.6. Strive for a consistent level of detail at each level in the hierarchy.

Functions can appear in any order in a program. But we shall follow the convention that the main function is the first one in a program, and all other functions are shown

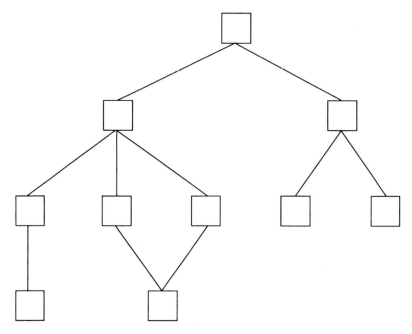

**Figure 4.6**   Functions which are called can themselves call other functions.

in alphabetical order by function name. This helps us to quickly understand what the program does and to quickly find any function. Without a logical order, a particular function could be hard to find in a large program.

A pre-condition states what must be true about a parameter variable on entry to a function. A post-condition states what must be true on exit from a function, provided all the pre-conditions have been met. A post-condition is a relationship between the parameter variables on entry and the parameter variables on exit from a function. A parameter variable on exit from a function is documented with the prime symbol, '. For example, the post-condition

```
/* post-condition: X' = X + Y */
```

says that the value of $X$ on exit from the function is equal the value of $X$ plus the value of $Y$ on entry to the function. Pre- and post-conditions form the basis of a contract between a function and its user. If the user does not meet the pre-conditions, then the behaviour of the function is not defined – we cannot guarantee that the function will behave as required. Every function should have its pre- and post-conditions specified along with its prototype; this informs the person reading or using the function about its purpose and how it should be used.

Programmer defined type identifiers should begin with an upper-case letter. Functions which return a value should have an identifer which describes the nature of that value. Functions which do not explicitly return a value should have an identifer which describes the function's purpose. For example, *int sumOfTwoNumers(int X, int Y)* returns the sum of two numbers, but *void addTwoNumbers(int X, int Y, int \*Z)* adds two numbers and places the result in \*Z.

If a function does not explicitly return a value, but returns a value (or values) in its parameters, then place them at the end of the parameter list, as shown in *addTwoNumbers* above.

If a function is to be used in just one, specific situation, then choose parameter names which are the same as the argument names. If a function is a general-purpose one, to be used in several different contexts, then use general-purpose parameter names (which are not necessarily the same as the argument names).

## 4.7   Programming Principles

Design your programs so that

- a main control function which defines the whole of **what** is to be done
- they are made up of a hierarchy of functions
- each function does one small task
- each function has a well-defined interface, that is, parameter list
- values are passed between functions only through their interface and return values

Make each function as self-contained as possible. Pass the minimum number of argument values from one function to another, that is, just enough to do the job.

If you have a choice of either explicitly returning a value from a function or passing an address as an argument to a parameter variable, return the value; this is simpler and less prone to error.

Provide pre- and post-conditions for every function you write. Whenever you make a call to a function, remember that it is up to you to ensure that its pre-conditions are met.

*Exercise 4.2*

**Remember to document your functions with pre- and post-conditions, and to document your programs with structure charts.**

1 A veterinary surgeon charges farmers on the basis of hours spent treating an animal, from the moment the vet leaves his or her home to the moment the vet returns. The vet charges to the nearest hour and the minimum charge is for one hour's work. Design, write and test a function, which is to be part of a billing program, which has parameters for the hours worked and rate per hour, and which returns the charge payable.
2 A garden centre orders bags of compost to replace those sold in the past month. Design, write and test a function which is to be part of an automated re-order system. The function is to have parameters for the number of bags sold in the past month and the maximum number of bags that can be stored on the premises. The function is to return the number of bags to be re-ordered.

**3** Design, write and test a function to be used in a college timetabling program. The function is to have parameters for room capacity and anticipated number of students in a class. The function is to return whether the class will fit in the room.

**4** A hotel guest is charged extra for certain goods and services. The extra charge is added to the guest's bill. A function is required which will be part of a billing program. The function is to have parameters for the current bill, the cost of extra services and the percentage service charge to be added to every goods or services provided. The function is to return the new, increased bill.

**5** Design, write and test function named doubleLessThan. The function is to have three parameters of type double and is to return TRUE if the first parameter is less than the second or FALSE if the second parameter is less than the first, within the tolerance specified by the third parameter.

**6** Design, write and test a function named doubleGreaterThan. The function should use doubleEqual and doubleLessThan in its implementation.

**7** Design and write a program which can be used to calculate an employee's gross pay. The program is to input the standard and overtime rates of pay per hour, and the number of hours actually worked in a week. The standard hours worked in a week is to be held as an enumerated constant set to, typically, 37. Any hours worked in excess of 37 is to be counted as overtime. The program is to calculate and output the gross pay.

**8** Design and write a program which might be used by the local constabulary to help determine whether a suspect for a crime is worth investigating further. The program is to input a suspects details – whether or not they have a motive, past form or an alibi – and to output whether or not the suspect meets any two of the three criteria: has a motive, has past form or has no alibi.

**9** Design and write a program which might be used by a friendship agency. The program is to input details of two clients – their name, age and whether they prefer to spend their time outdoors or within the home and garden; the program is to output whether the two clients might make a suitable match. A match is made if the two clients' ages are within five years of each other and they both share the same interests.

**10** Design and write a program which might be used by a book publisher to help determine the cost of editing, printing and publishing a book. The cost of editing an author's typescript and producing camera-ready copy is about £5.00 per page. The cost of printing is about £2.00 for each 250 (or part of 250) pages. The cost of binding and distribution is about £2.00 per book. The program is to input the number of pages in a book, the number of books to be printed, and the costs of editing and producing camera-ready pages, printing, binding and distribution. The program is to output the total cost of editing, printing and publishing the book.

# 5

# Iterations

## 5.1  Introduction

A computer can perform the same task many times without human intervention.
Suppose we want to print the word *GO* three times. We could write

```
printf(" GO");
printf(" GO");
printf(" GO");
printf("!");
```

But if we want to print the word *GO* one hundred times, then this approach is a
little tedious. We need a better method. Such a method is used in the following
program.

```
/* program 5.1 - prints GO 3 times. */


#include <stdio.h>


void main(void)
{
   int i = 0;

   while (i < 3) {
      printf(" GO");
      i = i + 1;
   }
   printf("!\n");
}
```

When executed, this program prints

```
GO GO GO!
```

on the screen.

How does it work? Initially, the variable *i* contains the value zero. *i* is less than three and so *GO* is printed and *i* is increased by one; *i* now contains one. *i* is still less than three and so *GO* is printed and *i* is increased by one; *i* now contains two. *i* is still less than three and so *GO* is printed and *i* is increased by one; *i* now contains three. *i* is not less than three and so the exclamation mark is printed.

So, for as long as (that is, while) the Boolean expression *(i < 3)* remains TRUE, *GO* is printed and the value held in *i* is increased by one. Eventually, there comes a time when the Boolean expression *(i < 3)* is not TRUE; then the *!* is printed and the program terminates.

Repeatedly executing a group of statements is known as a looping. Figure 5.1 shows why.

```
          int i = 0;

          ►while (i < 3) {      if (i < 3) is not TRUE then skip to here,
loop          printf(" GO");      otherwise go straight on.
              i = i + 1;
          }
          printf("!\n");
```

**Figure 5.1**   The two statements printf(" GO") and i = i + 1 are repeatedly executed for as long as i remains less than 3.

The construct

```
while (i < 3) {
    ...
}
```

is an example of an iteration. An iteration construct is used whenever a sequence of statements is to be repeatedly executed. An iteration construct is also known as a loop or repetition construct.

## 5.2   Simple Validation

Students are asked to rate, on a scale from 0 (appalling) to 5 (excellent), the quality of food supplied by the refectory. The results of the survey are to be held in a computer system for subsequent analysis – but we shall not go into that here. However, it is important that only values within the range 0–5 inclusive are stored. So, if a value outside this range is entered, then the user is again invited to enter an appropriate value; this is repeated until a value between 0 and 5 inclusive is entered.

To input one value is straightforward.

```
rating = intNumberRead(
                "Rating on a scale of 0 to 5 inclusive? ");
```

We need to determine whether the number entered is within the required range.

```
isInRange(rating, 0, 5);
```

If the number is not in the required range, we invite the user to re-enter the rating and check whether the number entered is within the required range.

```
if (!isInRange(rating, 0, 5)) {
   printf(
        "Please choose a value between 0 and 5 only.\n");
   rating = intNumberRead("Rating? ");
}
```

We need to repeatedly execute these last two statements for as long as the number entered remains out of range.

```
while (!isInRange(rating, 0, 5)) {
   printf(
        "Please choose a value between 0 and 5 only.\n");
   rating = intNumberRead("Rating? ");
}
```

Putting it all together we get

```
int rating = intNumberRead(
                "Rating on a scale of 0 to 5 inclusive? ");

while (!isInRange(rating, 0, 5)) {
   printf(
        "Please choose a value between 0 and 5 only.\n");
   rating = intNumberRead("Rating? ");
}

printf("Thank you.\n");
```

The complete program is given on the next page.

```
/* program 5.2 - simple validation. */

#include <stdio.h>


int intNumberRead(char prompt[]);
/* post-condition: returns number entered at the
keyboard. */


int isInRange(int value, int min, int max);
/* returns 1 if min <= value <= max, otherwise returns 0. */


void main(void)
{
   int rating = intNumberRead(
               "Rating on a scale of 0 to 5 inclusive? ");

   while (!isInRange(rating, 0, 5)) {
     printf(
          "Please choose a value between 0 and 5 only.\n");
     rating = intNumberRead("Rating? ");
   }
   printf("Thank you.\n");
}

int intNumberRead(char prompt[])
{
   char string[BUFSIZ];
   int number = 0;

   printf("%s", prompt);
   gets(string);
   sscanf(string, "%d", &number);
   return number;
}


int isInRange(int value, int min, int max)
{
   return ((min <= value) && (value <= max));
}
```

Two examples of program runs are

```
(1)   Rating on a scale of 0 to 5 inclusive? -1
      Please choose a value between 0 and 5 only.
      Rating on a scale of 0 to 5? 0
      Thank you.

(2)   Rating on a scale of 0 to 5 inclusive? 6
      Please choose a value between 0 and 5 only.
      Rating on a scale of 0 to 5 inclusive? 5
      Thank you.
```

## 5.3   Summing a Sequence of Numbers

A point-of-sale terminal in a supermarket is used to input the price of each item in pence (data entry is quicker if the decimal point is not entered) and to add the price to a running total. When zero is entered (for example, by pressing the return key alone), the total to be paid by the customer is displayed.

We consider three cases:

(a) before any item is entered
(b) when only one item is entered
(c) when several items are entered.

(a) Before any item is entered, we expect the running total to be zero.

```
long runningTotal = 0L;
```

(b) When one item is entered, we add its cost to the running total but only if the cost is not zero.

```
costOfItem = longNumberRead("Price? ");
if (costOfItem != 0L)
   runningTotal = runningTotal + costOfItem;
```

(c) But when several items are entered, we repeatedly add the cost of each item to the running total provided the cost of an item is not zero.

```
costOfItem = longNumberRead("Price? ");
while (costOfItem != 0L) {
   runningTotal = runningTotal + costOfItem;
   costOfItem = longNumberRead("Price? ");
}
```

Items are entered for as long as the cost of an item is not zero.

Putting the three cases together we obtain

```
long runningTotal = 0L;
long costOfItem = longNumberRead("Price? ");

while (costOfItem != 0L) {
   runningTotal = runningTotal + costOfItem;
   costOfItem = longNumberRead("Price? ");
}
```

Here is a simple program which simulates a point-of-sale terminal.

```
/* program 5.3 - point of sale simulation. */

#include <stdio.h>

long longNumberRead(char prompt[]);
/* post-condition: returns the number entered at the   */
/* keyboard.                                            */


void main(void)
{
   long runningTotal = 0L;
   long costOfItem = longNumberRead("Price? ");

   while (costOfItem != 0L) {
      runningTotal = runningTotal + costOfItem;
      costOfItem = longNumberRead("Price? ");
   }
   printf("Total bill is £%0.2f\n", runningTotal/100.0);
}


long longNumberRead(char prompt[])
{
   char string[BUFSIZ];
   long number = 0L;

   printf("%s", prompt);
   gets(string);
   sscanf(string, "%ld", &number);
   return number;
}
```

Here are three examples of program runs.

```
(1)   Price? 89
      Price? 89
      Price? 79
      Price? 179
      Price? 0
      The balance due is £4.36

(2)   Price? 100
      Price? 0
      The balance due is £1.00

(3)   Price? 0
      The balance due is £0.00
```

## 5.4  Printing a Table

A boat company offers four-berth boats for hire for up to six days at a time. An example of their hire charges is shown in the table below.

Boat Hire Charges 1994

| Period | Charge |
|--------|--------|
| 1 day  | £10.00 |
| 2 days | £20.00 |
| 3 days | £30.00 |
| 4 days | £40.00 |
| 5 days | £50.00 |
| 6 days | £60.00 |

We are to design a program which will input a daily charge and output the table. We consider four cases:

(a) before any entries for any one day is printed
(b) a table with just one entry for one day
(c) a table with two entries for two days
(d) a table with six entries.

(a) Before any entries are printed we input the daily charge and print the headings.

```
costPerDay = doubleNumberRead("Charge per day? ");
printf("BOAT HIRE CHARGES 1994\n\n");
printf("Period     Charge\n\n");
```

(b)  To print just one entry we print the first line of the table.

```
dayNumber = 1;
printf("%d day    £%2.2f\n", dayNumber, costPerDay);
```

(c)  To print the next entry we add one to *dayNumber* and print the second line of the table.

```
dayNumber = dayNumber + 1;
printf("%d days    £%2.2f\n", dayNumber, costPerDay);
```

(d)  We print the last line when *dayNumber* contains six.

```
dayNumber = dayNumber + 1;
while (dayNumber < 7) {
   printf("%d days    £%0.2f\n", dayNumber, costPerDay *
                                              dayNumber);
   dayNumber = dayNumber + 1;
}
```

The following program inputs the hire charge for one day and then prints the table on the screen.

```
/* program 5.4 - prints a table of hire charges. */

#include <stdio.h>

double doubleNumberRead(char prompt[]);

void main(void)
{
   double costPerDay = doubleNumberRead("Charge per day? £");
   int dayNumber = 1;

   printf("\nBOAT HIRE CHARGES 1994\n\n");
   printf("Period     Charge\n\n");
   printf("%d day       £%0.2f\n", dayNumber, costPerDay);
   dayNumber = dayNumber + 1;
   while (dayNumber < 7) {
      printf("%d days       %0.2f\n", dayNumber, costPerDay *
                                                 dayNumber);
      dayNumber = dayNumber + 1;
   }
}
```

```
double doubleNumberRead(char prompt[])
{
   char string[BUFSIZ];
   double number = 0.0;

   printf("%s", prompt);
   gets(string);
   sscanf(string, "%lf", &number);
   return number;
}
```

An example of a program run is

```
Daily charge? £10

Boat Hire Charges 1994

Period   Charge

1 day    £10.00
2 days   £20.00
3 days   £30.00
4 days   £40.00
5 days   £50.00
6 days   £60.00
```

## 5.5  Designing a Loop Construct

We illustrate the principles with an example. We are required to design and write a program which will provide examination statistics for an unspecified number of students. We are required to provide statistics showing the total number of students who sat an examination and, of those, how many passed. The examination marks are in the range 0–100 and a pass is awarded to each mark which is 50 or more.

First, we establish the initial conditions by looking at the case when the number of students who sat the exam is zero.

```
int studentsPassed = 0;     Solution for totalStudents == 0
int studentsProcessed = 0;
```

Then, using this solution, we obtain the solution for the case when only one student sat the exam.

*Solution for totalStudents == 1*
```
int examinationMark = intNumberRead("Mark? ");

if (examinationMark >= passMark)
    studentsPassed = studentsPassed + 1;

studentsProcessed = studentsProcessed + 1;
```

But we do not know how many students sat the exam. We need to be able to determine when there are no more examination marks to be entered. Since an examination mark is between 0 and 100 inclusive, we could use a mark of −1 to mean no more input. So we write

```
examinationMark = intNumberRead("Mark? ");
while (examinationMark != -1) {
   if (examinationMark >= passMark)
      studentsPassed = studentsPassed + 1;
   studentsProcessed = studentsProcessed + 1;
   examinationMark = intNumberRead("Mark? ");
}
```

The completed design is

```
enum { passMark = 50 };

int studentsPassed = 0;
int studentsProcessed = 0;

examinationMark = intNumberRead("Mark? ");
while (examinationMark != -1) {
   if (examinationMark >= passMark)
      studentsPassed = studentsPassed + 1;
   studentsProcessed = studentsProcessed + 1;
   examinationMark = intNumberRead("Mark? ");
}

writeTotals(studentsProcessed, studentsPassed);
```

Check:

- when there are no students and the mark entered is −1, the loop is not executed and both *studentsPassed* and *studentsProcessed* are zero
- when one student's mark is entered, the loop is executed once only and *studentsProcessed* is one.

That completes the design process.
   Incidentally, we could replace

```
studentsPassed = studentsPassed + 1;
```

with

```
studentsPassed++;
```

*++* is known as the increment operator; it increases the value stored in an integer variable by one.

## 5.6   Documentation

Statements to be repeatedly executed are indented by two character spaces under the *while* keyword. A block of statements to be repeatedly executed is enclosed within braces positioned as shown below.

*while (boolean-expression) {*
   *statement-1;*
   *statement-2;*
   *...*
   *statement-n;*
*}*

## 5.7   Programming Principles

Use a loop whenever a sequence of statements is to be repeatedly executed.

Remember to use a function such as *doubleEqual* if you must use *double* (or *float*) values in Boolean expressions which control the execution of a loop; equality of values of type *float* or *double* is not always easy to determine – see Chapter 4 for example.

Always provide simple validation of user input. Remember that it is up to you, the programmer, to ensure that valid values are passed to function parameters no matter what the user does. A value is valid if it falls between some pre-determined limits.

Always check that a loop behaves correctly for zero repetitions, one repetition and the maximum number of repetitions. Your loops should execute the required number of times exactly, not one more, not one less. When testing a loop, consider choosing data values which cause the loop

(a)   not to be executed at all
(b)   to be executed once only
(c)   to be executed the maximum number of times.

*Exercise 5.1*

**1** Design a loop which will print a horizontal line of ten asterisks. Then test your design in a simple program.
**2** Design a loop which will print the 13-times table up to 12 × 13. Then write a program to test your design.
**3** Write and test a function which will input a person's age in years. If the age input is less than zero or more than 110 then output the message "Don't be silly!" and invite the user to input a person's age again; this is to be repeated until the age input lies between 0 and 110. The function is to return an age between 0 and 110 inclusive.

**4** Write a program which will input the wages for an unspecified number of employees and output the total wage bill, the number of employees whose wage has been input and the average wage. If the number of employees is zero, your program should display a suitable message if the number of employees is zero and not calculate the average wage (why?).

**5** A waste removal company offers skips for hire on a daily or weekly basis. The weekly charge is six times the daily charge. Write a program which will input the daily charge and output a table of charges in the following format:

| Time period | Charge |
| --- | --- |
| 1 day | |
| 2 days | |
| ... | |
| 6 days | |
| 1 week | |
| 2 weeks | |
| ... | |
| 4 weeks | |

**6** The value of a computer system depreciates by 50% of its current value at the beginning of each year of its life.  For example, suppose a system was purchased for £1000, then immediately its value would be £500.  After 12 months, its value would be £250 and one year after that its value would be £125. Write a program which will

(a)  input the purchase price of a computer system
(b)  write a table showing its value at the beginning of each year of ownership for five years
(c)  output the first year in which its value is less than 20% of its purchase price.

# 6
# Arrays

## 6.1 Introduction

We have already met definitions similar to

```
char string[10];
```

This defines an object named string which has ten consecutive containers numbered from zero up to nine.

string

|   |   |   |   |   |   |   |   |   |   |
|---|---|---|---|---|---|---|---|---|---|
| 0 | 1 | 2 | 3 | 4 | 5 | 6 | 7 | 8 | 9 |

*string* is an example of an array. An array is a set of contiguous containers, that is, each container is joined to its neighbour and there are no gaps between them. The number of containers in an array is known as its size. An array with size equal to ten has containers numbered from zero up to nine inclusive.

If we initialised the array *string* thus

```
char string[10] = "Mr Smilly";
```

then one character is stored in each container.

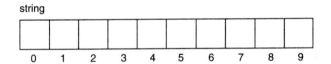

string

| M | r |   | S | m | i | l | l | y | \0 |
|---|---|---|---|---|---|---|---|---|----|
| 0 | 1 | 2 | 3 | 4 | 5 | 6 | 7 | 8 | 9  |

\0 represents the end-of-string marker known as the *NULL* character. It is automatically placed in the array by the compiler when an array of characters is initialised in this way (provided, of course, there is enough room in the array).

Each container in an array is known as an element. Each element number is known as an index or subscript. Each element of an array is referenced by enclosing its index within square brackets thus

```
string[0], string[1], string[2], ... string[9].
```

The value stored in *string[3]* is 'S'. *string[8]* contains 'y'. *string[10]* does not exist. To store the value 'e' in *string[5]* we write

```
string[5] = 'e';
```

This overwrites the value previously stored in *string[5]*.

string

| M | r |   | S | m | e | l | l | y | \0 |
|---|---|---|---|---|---|---|---|---|----|
| 0 | 1 | 2 | 3 | 4 | 5 | 6 | 7 | 8 | 9  |

All the values stored in an array must be of the same type. In *string* for example, every element contains a value of type *char*. So, string is an array of type *char*.

Arrays can store values of other types such as *int*, *float* and enumerated values.

## 6.2   The Length of a String

In C, a string is a sequence of characters, terminated with the *NULL* character (denoted by \0). A string may be held in an array of type *char*. The library named *string* contains functions which enable us to determine the number of characters actually held in an array of *char* and to copy the contents of one *char* array into another. Let us see how these may be used and implemented.

The following program finds the length of a string input by the user.

```
/* program 6.1 - finds the length of a string. */

#include <stdio.h>
#include <string.h>


void main(void)
{
  char string[BUFSIZ];
  unsigned long lengthOfString;
```

```
printf("String? ");
gets(string);
lengthOfString = (unsigned long)strlen(string);
printf("Length of string entered is %lu",
                                    lengthOfString);
}
```

An example of a program run is

```
String? abcde
Length of string entered is 5
```

*abcde* would be stored in the array like this

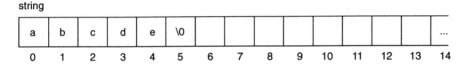

What is stored in elements 6 onwards is not defined. *strlen* counts the number of characters up to (but not including) the first *NULL* character; this number is known as the length of the string. Let us look at some of the details in program 6.1.

*string.h* contains the prototype for the function *strlen*. The line

```
lengthOfString = (unsigned long)strlen(string);
```

says store the length of *string* in *lengthOfString*. The cast operator *(unsigned long)* ensures that a value of the right type is assigned to *lengthOfString*.

It is instructive to see how *strlen* might be implemented. Our version of *strlen*, named *stringLength* and shown below, returns the number of characters in a string up to, but not including, the *NULL* character.

```
unsigned stringLength(char string[])
/* pre-condition:   string contains a NULL-terminated */
/*                  sequence of characters.           */
/* post-condition:  returns the number of characters  */
/*                  in string.                         */
{
    unsigned length = 0u;

    while (string[length] != NULL)
        length++;
    return length;
}
```

If *string* contains no characters (apart from the *NULL* character) the loop is not executed at all and zero is returned. If *string* contains two characters, the first being a non-*NULL* character and the second the *NULL* character, the loop is executed once and length is incremented (that is, increased by one). One is returned.

## 6.3  Copying a String

From time to time we need to make a copy of all or part of a string. *strncpy* from the string library copies a number of characters from one string to another. Its use is illustrated in program 6.2.

```
/* program 6.2 - copies a string. */


#include <stdio.h>
#include <string.h>


void copyNChars(const char string[], unsigned nChars,
                char newString[]);
/* pre-condition:   string contains a null-terminated   */
/*                  sequence of characters.             */
/* post-condition:  copies nChars from string into       */
/*                  newString, appends NULL to newString.*/


void main(void)
{
   char string[BUFSIZ], newString[BUFSIZ];

   printf("String? ");
   gets(string);
   copyNChars(string, 5, newString);
   printf("The new string is %s", newString);
}

void copyNChars(const char source[], unsigned nChars,
                                    char destination[])
{
   strncpy(destination, source, nChars);
   destination[nChars] = NULL;
}
```

Three examples of program runs are

(1)   String? **abcd**
      The new string is abcd

(2)   String? **abcde**
      The new string is abcde

(3)   String? **abcdef**
      The new string is abcde

Inside *main*, we have defined two arrays of type *char*.

```
char string[BUFSIZ], newString[BUFSIZ];
```

To pass an array as an argument value to a function parameter, we supply just its name. Here, the arrays *string* and *newString* are passed to *copyNChars*.

```
copyNChars(string, 5, newString);
```

However, what is actually passed is the address of the first element of the array; this is done automatically by C.
   In the function declaration

```
void copyNChars(const char source[], unsigned nChars,
                                 char destination[])
```

the array parameters are written *char source[]* and *char destination[]*. The empty brackets *[ ]* indicate that both *source* and *destination* are to contain the start address of an array.
   Now, if a function parameter contains the address of a variable, then the function can change the contents of that variable. To prevent this from happening, the keyword *const* is used to qualify the parameter. The contents of arrays marked as *const* remain constant during function execution.
   In the function call

```
strncpy(destination, source, nChars);
```

*nChars* are copied from *source* into *destination*. Suppose *nChars* contains five. If source contains "*abc*", then *abc* is copied into *destination* followed by two *NULL* characters to make up the five. If *source* contains "*abcdef*" then just the first five characters are copied into *destination*; a terminating *NULL* character is **not** copied into the array, as shown in the diagram on the next page.

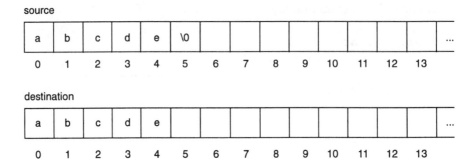

Since the terminating *NULL* character is required by many functions which have string parameters, it is up to us as programmers to ensure that any string we create is properly terminated. That is why we write

```
destination[nChars] = NULL;
```

in

```
void copyNChars(const char source[], unsigned nChars,
                                      char destination[])
{
    strncpy(destination, source, nChars);
    destination[nChars] = NULL;
}
```

Here we have used *nChars* to represent a number of characters **and** a container number; they are not the same thing. We need to place the terminating *NULL* character in the element numbered 5 in the destination array.

The destination array must be sufficiently large to contain the expected number of characters, otherwise, the behaviour of *strncpy* is undefined.

To display the contents of an array of *char*, i.e. a string, *%s* is used as the conversion specification in *printf*.

```
printf("The new string is %s", newString);
```

## 6.4  Testing a Character

Since we are dealing with arrays of characters, it may be reasonable at this point to examine characters a little more closely.

Sometimes we need to know whether a character is a letter or a space or a digit. Let us design a function which will count the number of spaces in a string.

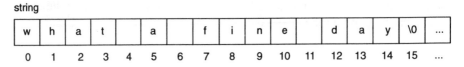

Essentially, the method is: move through the array from its beginning up to the first *NULL* character inspecting the contents of each container as you go; if the value stored in a container is a space, then increment a number-of-spaces counter. Here is the function.

```
unsigned numberOfSpacesInString(const char string[])
{
   unsigned spaceCount = 0u;
   unsigned i = 0u;

   while (string[i] != NULL) {
      if (isspace(string[i]))
         spaceCount++;
      i++;
   }
   return spaceCount;
}
```

*i* refers to each element number in the array. It starts off with the value zero. Then, for as long as the character stored in the location numbered *i* is not the *NULL* character, if the location contains the space character, then increment *spaceCount*; move onto the next location. Finally, return the value stored in *spaceCount*.

*isspace* is defined in *ctype.h*. *isspace* returns one (i.e. TRUE) if its *char* argument is the space character, otherwise is returns zero (i.e. FALSE).

Here is a complete program which uses the function.

```
/* program 6.3 - counts spaces in a string. */

#include <stdio.h>
#include <ctype.h>

unsigned numberOfSpacesInString(const char string[]);
/*   pre:   string is a null-terminated sequence of */
/*          characters.                             */
/*   post: returns the number of spaces in string. */

void main(void)
{
   char string[BUFSIZ];
   unsigned nSpaces;

   printf("String? ");
   gets(string);
   nSpaces = numberOfSpacesInString(string);
   printf("The number of spaces in the string is %u", nSpaces);
}
```

```
unsigned numberOfSpacesInString(const char string[])
{
  unsigned spaceCount = 0u;
  unsigned i = 0u;


  while (string[i] != NULL) {
    if (isspace(string[i]))
      spaceCount++;
    i++;
  }
  return spaceCount;
}
```

An example of a program run is

```
String? What a fine day it is today.
Number of spaces in the string is 6
```

*isspace* is a function which returns TRUE if its character argument is the space character, otherwise, it returns FALSE. Other functions which work in a similar way are *isalpha* (checks whether a character is a letter), *isdigit* (checks whether a character is a digit) and *islower* (checks whether a character is a lower-case character). The prototypes for these functions are found *in ctype.h*.


## 6.5   The Case Sensitivity Problem

Also defined in *ctype* is the function *toupper*. *toupper* converts a lower-case character to its upper-case equivalent. Here is its specification.

```
int toupper(int ch);
/* post-condition: returns upper-case equivalent of ch */
/*                  if ch is a lower-case letter,       */
                    otherwise returns ch unchanged.     */
```

Notice that the implied pre-condition is that the argument value is an *int* and that the function returns an *int*. In C, values of type *char* can be stored in *int* variables. This is necessary because some character values, such as the end-of-file character, cannot be stored in a *char* variable. But this need not concern us here.

C is case sensitive. So the two string literals *Smith* and *SMITH* are not the same. In some circumstances we would want *Smith* and *SMITH* to represent the same item. So we need a function which will convert all the lower-case characters in a string to upper case. Here is the specification of such a function.

```
void convertStringToUpperCase(const char string[],
                                    char upperCaseString[]);
/* pre-condition:   string is a NULL-terminated sequence */
/*                  of characters.                        */
/* post-condition: upperCaseString' contains the upper   */
/*                  case equivalent of string.            */
```

An example of a call to this function is

```
char name[BUFSIZ], upperCaseName[BUFSIZ];

readString("Enter name: ", name);
convertStringToUpperCase(name, upperCaseName);
```

The implementation of *convertStringToUpperCase* is straightforward. Go through string from beginning to end: for each character in string, obtain its upper case equivalent and place it in *upperCaseString*.

```
void convertStringToUpperCase(const char string[],
                                    char upperCaseString[])
{
  int i = 0;

  while (string[i] != NULL) {
    upperCaseString[i] = (char)toupper(string[i]);
    i++;
  }
  upperCaseString[i] = NULL;
}
```

*Exercise 6.1*

1 Many telephone numbers contain 11-digit characters. Spaces are allowed between groups of digits and sometimes a group of digits is contained within brackets. Write a function which has a string argument and returns whether (or not) the string contains 11 digits.
2 A telephone number is perhaps best stored in two arrays, one for the area code and one for the number. Write a function which receives a full telephone number in one parameter and returns the number in its two constituent parts in two other parameters.
3 Write a program to test the *convertStringToUpperCase* function described in section 6.5.

**4** Design, write and test a function called stringEqual. The function is to have two string parameters and is to return one if the two parameter values are the same; otherwise it is to return zero. The function should use the *strcmp* function defined in the *string* library. Its specification is

```
int strcmp(const char s1[], const char s2[]);
/* Compares two strings character by character until either
two characters are found which are not identical or the end
of a string is reached. Returns a number less than zero if
the first character of the pair comes before the second one
in "character table order", returns a number greater than
zero if the first character of the pair comes after the second
one, returns zero if the two strings are identical. */
```

A commonly used "character table" is the American Standard Code for Information Interchange (ASCII) table. Part of this table is shown below.

<space> 0 1 2 3 4 5 6 7 8 9
A B C D E F G H I J K L M N O P Q R S T U V W X Y Z
a b c d e f g h i j k l m n o p q r s t u v w x y z

So, for example, A comes before B in ASCII table order sequence but a does not come before B.

The ASCII collating (i.e. character ordering) sequence is similar to, but not the same as, alphabetical or dictionary order. In dictionary order, the letters would be ordered like this

A a B b C c D d ...

So perhaps the argument values to *strcmp* should be upper-case strings. An example of a call to *strcmp* is

```
char string1[BUFSIZ], string2[BUFSIZ];
char upperCaseString1[BUFSIZ], upperCaseString2[BUFSIZ];

readString("String? ", string1);
readString("Another string? ", string2);
convertStringToUpperCase(string1, upperCaseString1);
convertStringToUpperCase(string2, upperCaseString2);
if (strcmp(upperCaseString1, upperCaseString2)) == 0)
  printf("Equal\n");
else if strcmp(upperCaseString1, upperCaseString2)) < 0)
  printf("First string comes before the second.\n");
else if strcmp(upperCaseString1, upperCaseString2)) > 0)
  printf("first string comes after the second.\n");
```

**5** Write a function which will return TRUE if the first of its two string arguments comes before the second in dictionary order, or FALSE if otherwise. So, for example, if the function was named *stringLessThan*

```
stringLessThan("apple", "zoo") == TRUE;
stringLessThan("zoo", "apple") == FALSE;
```

**6** Nearly every new book published is assigned an International Standard Book Number (ISBN); no two books have the same ISBN. An ISBN contains ten digits; the last one is the check digit. An example of an ISBN is 0131103628. In this example, the check digit is 8.

The check digit is calculated from the first nine digits using the modulus 11 weighted method, as shown in the following example.

First, each digit is multiplied by its weight starting with 10.

| partISBN | 0 | 1 | 3 | 1 | 1 | 0 | 3 | 6 | 2 |
|---|---|---|---|---|---|---|---|---|---|
| weight | ×10 | ×9 | ×8 | ×7 | ×6 | ×5 | ×4 | ×3 | ×2 |
| partSum | 0 | 9 | 24 | 7 | 6 | 0 | 12 | 18 | 4 |

Then the part sums are totalled.

total = 0 + 9 + 24 + 7 + 6 + 0 + 12 + 18 + 4 = 80

Then the total is divided by 11 to obtain the remainder.

80/11 = 7 remainder 3

The remainder is subtracted from 11 to obtain the checkDigit.

checkDigit = 11 − 3 = 8

If the checkDigit turns out to be 10, then X is used to represent it.

Write a program which contains the following functions:

```
void getISBN(char ISBN[]);
/* post-condition: ISBN' contains a NULL terminated    */
/*                 ISBN number entered at the keyboard. */

char checkDigitFromISBN(const char ISBN[]);
/* pre-condition:  ISBN is a NULL-terminated sequence */
/*                 of digit characters.               */
/* post-condition: returns the last digit (or letter) */
/*                 character contained in ISBN.        */
```

```
void getPartISBNFromISBN(const char ISBN[],
                                      char PartISBN[]);
/* pre-condition:  ISBN contains a NULL terminated   */
/*                 ISBN number.                       */
/* post-condition: PartISBN' contains all the digit  */
/*                 characters contained in ISBN except*/
/*                 the check digit character.         */


char calculatedCheckDigit(const char PartISBN[]);
/* pre-condition:  PartISBN contains all the digit   */
/*                 characters in an ISBN except for   */
/*                 the check digit character.         */
/* post-condition: returns the check digit calculated */
/*                 from the PartISBN using the modulus*/
/*                 11 weighted method.                */



int checkDigitsAreEqual(char calculatedCheckDigit,
                                    char theCheckDigit);
/* post-condition: returns TRUE if                    */
/*                 calculatedCheckDigit = theCheckDigit,*/
/*                 otherwise, returns FALSE.          */
```

Your program should input ten characters to represent an ISBN number. The program should then calculate, from the first nine-digit characters entered, what the check digit should be. Then your program should compare the check digit entered with the one calculated; if they are different the program should output "The number entered is not a valid ISBN", otherwise, the program should output "ISBN is OK". You might find the following two functions useful

```
unsigned digitFromCharacter(char ch)
/* pre-condition:  char is a digit character.         */
/* post-condition: returns the number equivalent of ch.*/
/* If ch contains the character '8' then              */
/* digitFromCharacter returns the integer 8. The      */
/* normal arithmetic operations can be performed on   */
/* unsigned int values. (We do not normally perform   */
/* arithmetic with chars.)  An example of a call to   */
/* this function is                                   */
/* integerDigit = digitFromCharacter(partISBN[index]); */
{
    return (unsigned)ch - '0';
}
```

```
char characterFromDigit(unsigned digit)
/* pre-condition:  digit is one of 0,1,2,3,4,5,6,7,8,9*/
/* post-condition: returns the character equivalent of*/
/*                 digit.                              */
/* characterFromDigit is the converse of              */
/* digitFromCharacter.                                 */
/* An example of a call to this function is            */
/* checkDigitCharacter = characterFromDigit(checkDigit); */
{
    return (char)digit + '0';
}
```

**7** Design, write and test a function which will convert an unsigned integer number into a string.

## 6.6  Arrays of Numbers

A financial director wishes to know the largest salary in a group of salaries. Suppose the salaries are contained in an array.

salaries

| 18000 | 17500 | 23750 | 14275 | 16000 | 12500 | 19000 |
|-------|-------|-------|-------|-------|-------|-------|
| 0     | 1     | 2     | 3     | 4     | 5     | 6     |

How can we find the largest value in the array? We look at the contents of the first container; it is the largest salary seen so far. Then we look at the contents of each of the following containers in turn: if we find a salary which is larger than the one seen so far, then that salary becomes the largest seen so far.

```
double largestSalaryInSalaries(double salaries[],
                                      unsigned lastIndex)
{
   unsigned i = 0u;
   double largestSalary = salaries[i];

   while (i <= lastIndex) {
     if (salaries[i] > largestSalary)
       largestSalary = salaries[i];
     i++;
   }
   return largestSalary;
}
```

We are obliged to let the *largestSalaryInSalaries* function know what the last array index value is because, otherwise, it would have no way of knowing where the array ends. It would be an error if we attempted to refer to an element which does not exist. So, for example, we do not use index *i* if it contains a value greater than *lastIndex*.

The next program, program 6.4, uses the *largestSalaryInSalaries* function.

```
/* program 6.4 - finds the largest value in an array of */
/*               numbers.                                */

#include <stdio.h>

void buildScenario(double salaries[]);
/* post-condition: salaries contains a sequence of       */
/*                 salary values.                        */

double largestSalaryInSalaries(const double salaries[],
                               unsigned lastIndex);
/* pre-condition:  lastIndex is the last index value     */
/*                 in salaries.                          */
/* post-condition: returns the largest value in salaries. */

void showLargestSalary(double salary);

void main(void)
{
   enum { lastIndex = 6u, arraySize = 7u };

   double salaries[arraySize];
   double largestSalary;

   buildScenario(salaries);
   largestSalary = largestSalaryInSalaries(salaries,
                                           lastIndex);
   showLargestSalary(largestSalary);
}

void buildScenario(double salaries[])
{
   salaries[0] = 18000;
   salaries[1] = 17500;
   salaries[2] = 23750;
   salaries[3] = 14275;
   salaries[4] = 16000;
   salaries[5] = 12500;
   salaries[6] = 19000;
}
```

```
double largestSalaryInSalaries(const double salaries[],
                                      unsigned lastIndex)
{
   unsigned i = 0;

   double largestSalary = salaries[i];

   while (i <= lastIndex) {
     if (salaries[i] > largestSalary)
       largestSalary = salaries[i];
     i++;
   }
   return largestSalary;
}

void showLargestSalary(double salary)
{
    printf("The largest salary is £%0.2f", salary);
}
```

When the program is executed

```
The largest salary is £23750.00
```

is shown on the screen.

First, let us look at *buildScenario*.

```
void buildScenario(double salaries[])
{
   salaries[0] = 18000;
   salaries[1] = 17500;
   salaries[2] = 23750;
   salaries[3] = 14275;
   salaries[4] = 16000;
   salaries[5] = 12500;
   salaries[6] = 19000;
}
```

In *buildScenario* we, as programmers, are storing explicit values in the array *salaries*. This means that these values do not have to be entered every time the program is run.

## 6.7 Arrays as Accumulators

Twenty college students were asked to rate the quality of food supplied by their refectory on a scale from zero (appalling) to five (excellent). The results are summarised in the following table:

Number of students who awarded 0 marks:  1

1 mark:   3

2 marks:   5

3 marks:   9

4 marks:   2

5 marks:   0

Out of the 20 students, only one gave zero marks for quality, three gave one mark for quality, five gave two marks, and so on. Can we use an array to hold the results of the poll? Yes we can, thus

students

| 1 | 3 | 5 | 9 | 2 | 0 |
|---|---|---|---|---|---|
| 0 | 1 | 2 | 3 | 4 | 5 |

Mark

The index values 0, 1, 2, 3, 4, and 5 represent each of the possible ratings of food quality. One student gave zero marks for food quality, three students gave one mark and five students gave two marks, and so on.

Initially, before the poll starts, no students have given any marks for the quality of food.

students

| 0 | 0 | 0 | 0 | 0 | 0 |
|---|---|---|---|---|---|
| 0 | 1 | 2 | 3 | 4 | 5 |

Mark

Suppose the first student polled awarded three marks. Then we need to increment students[3].

students

| 0 | 0 | 0 | 1 | 0 | 0 |
|---|---|---|---|---|---|
| 0 | 1 | 2 | 3 | 4 | 5 |

Mark

Suppose now that the second student polled also gave three marks for food quality. Then, again, we need to increment *students[3]*.

students

| 0 | 0 | 0 | 2 | 0 | 0 |
|---|---|---|---|---|---|
| 0 | 1 | 2 | 3 | 4 | 5 |

Mark

And again. Suppose the next student awarded two marks, then we need to increment *students[2]*.

students

| 0 | 0 | 1 | 2 | 0 | 0 |
|---|---|---|---|---|---|
| 0 | 1 | 2 | 3 | 4 | 5 |

Mark

So now we have a method for accumulating the marks awarded by the students for food quality. The function to accomplish the task is very simple:

```
void incrementStudentsWhoGaveMark(int mark, int students[])
{
    students[mark]++;
}
```

The line

```
students[mark]++;
```

increases the value contained in *students[mark]* by *1*. So, if *mark* contained *2* then the array container with index 2 has its value incremented.

Here is the complete program.

```
/* program 6.5 - analyses marks awarded for food quality.*/

#include <stdio.h>

void incrementStudentsWhoGaveMark(int mark, int students[]);
/* pre-condition:  mark is within the bounds of students. */
/* post-condition: students'[mark] = students[mark] + 1 */


void initialiseArray(int students[], int lastIndex);
/* post-condition: every element in students contains zero.*/

int intNumberRead(char prompt[]);
/* post-condition: returns the number entered at the      */
/*                      keyboard.                          */
```

```
int markRead(int min, int max);
/* post-condition: returns a value between min and max
inclusive. */


void showResults(const int students[], int lastIndex);


void main(void)
{
   enum { minMark = 0, maxMark = 5, lastIndex = 5,
        arraySize = 6, studentsPolled = 20 };


   int students[arraySize];
   int mark;
   int studentsProcessed = 0;


   initialiseArray(students, lastIndex);
   while (studentsProcessed < studentsPolled) {
      mark = markRead(minMark, maxMark);
      incrementStudentsWhoGaveMark(mark, students);
      studentsProcessed++;
   }
   showResults(students, lastIndex);
}


void incrementStudentsWhoGaveMark(int mark, int students[])
{
   students[mark]++;
}


void initialiseArray(int students[], int lastIndex)
{
   int i = 0;

   while (i <= lastIndex) {
      students[i] = 0;
      i++;
   }
}
```

```
int intNumberRead(char prompt[])
{
  char string[BUFSIZ];
  int number = 0;

  printf("%s", prompt);
  gets(string);
  sscanf(string, "%d", &number);
  return number;
}



int markRead(int min, int max)
{
  int mark = intNumberRead("Mark? ");

  while ((mark < min) || (mark > max)) {
    printf("The mark must lie between ");
    printf("%d and %d inclusive.\n", min, max);
    mark = intNumberRead("mark? ");
  }
  return mark;
}



void showResults(const int students[], int lastIndex)
{
  int mark = 0;

  printf("The results of the survey are: \n\n");
  printf("Grade    Number of Students\n\n");
  while (mark <= lastIndex) {
    printf("  %d                %d\n", mark, students[mark]);
    mark++;
  }
}
```

*Exercise 6.2*

1 Test program 6.5.
2 Create an array which contains the annual salary of about five employees. Then write and test functions which will find (a) the range of salaries (where we define range as being the largest salary minus the smallest salary) and (b) the average salary.

**3** Create an array which contains the number of days in each month for a non-leap year; store zero in the first array element so that index values ranging from 1 to 12 can be used to represent the month numbers.

daysInMonth

| 0 | 31 | 28 | 31 | 30 | 31 | 30 | 31 | 31 | 30 | 31 | 30 | 31 |
|---|----|----|----|----|----|----|----|----|----|----|----|----|
| 0 | 1  | 2  | 3  | 4  | 5  | 6  | 7  | 8  | 9  | 10 | 11 | 12 | month |

Then write a function (or functions) which will input a date in the form dayNumber, monthNumber.

An array which contains the days in each month can be used to check whether a dayNumber and a monthNumber can be a valid combination. For example, if day contains 31 and month contains 4 then day cannot be in month because there are only 30 days in April. Write and test a function to the following specification

```
int dayIsInMonth(int day, int month, const int daysInMonth[]);
/* pre-condition : month is in 0..12,                      */
/*                 daysInMonth contains the days in        */
/*                 each month and                          */
/*                 daysInMonth[0] contains zero.           */
/* post-condition: returns 1 if Day <=                     */
/*                 daysInMonth[month];                     */
/*                 otherwise returns 0.                    */
```

Now write and test a function which will convert a day in a month to a day in the year. For example, 1st January would be day 1 in the year, 2nd January would be day 2, 3rd January day 3, ... , 31st January day 31, 1st February day 32, ... and 31st December would be day 365 in the year. The 7th March would be day 66 (66 = 31 + 28 + 7) in the year. A specification for this function might be

```
int dayInYearNumber(int day, int month,
                         const int daysInMonth[]);
/* pre-condition:  dayIsInMonth(day, month)               */
/*                 daysInMonth contains the days in        */
/*                 each month and                          */
/*                 daysInMonth[0] contains zero.           */
/* post: returns day-in-year-number for day in month. */
```

## 6.8   Arrays of Strings

Suppose we need to store some names in an array. For example, suppose we need to store up to five names and that we allow up to 12 characters per name, then we need an array of five elements in which each element is itself an array of 13 elements.

Names

| | 0 | 1 | 2 | 3 | 4 | 5 | 6 | 7 | 8 | 9 | 10 | 11 | 12 |
|---|---|---|---|---|---|---|---|---|---|---|---|---|---|
| 0 | T | o | m | \0 | | | | | | | | | |
| 1 | D | i | c | k | \0 | | | | | | | | |
| 2 | H | a | r | r | y | \0 | | | | | | | |
| 3 | A | n | n | \0 | | | | | | | | | |
| 4 | M | a | y | \0 | | | | | | | | | |

We could define the type *String* as an array of 13 character elements.

```
typedef char String[13];
```

And then define the array of names as

```
String names[5];
```

This definition says that *names* is an array of five *String* elements (where a *String* element is itself an array of 13 character elements).

To print the contents of the array of strings is easy.

```
void printNames(const String names[], lastIndex)
{
   int i = 0;

   while (i <= lastIndex) {
      printf("%s \n", names[i]);
      i++;
   }
}
```

And to fill the array with names is just as easy.

```
void getNames(String names[], int lastIndex)
{
  int i = 0;

  while (i <= lastIndex) {
    printf("Name? ");
    gets(names[i]);
    i++;
  }
}
```

If *i* contains *2* and *names[i]* contains *Harry\0* then we can imagine the situation as shown in the picture below.

| 2 | H | a | r | r | y | \0 | | | | | | | |
|---|---|---|---|---|---|----|--|--|--|--|--|--|--|
| | 0 | 1 | 2 | 3 | 4 | 5 | 6 | 7 | 8 | 9 | 10 | 11 | 12 |

*names[2][0]* contains *'H'*, *names[2][4]* contains *'y'* and *names[2][5]* contains *'\0'*.
  Here is the complete program.

```
/* program 6.6 - arrays of fixed length strings. */

#include <stdio.h>
#include <string.h>

enum { stringSize = 13 };
typedef char String[stringSize];

void getNames(String names[], int lastIndex);
/* post-condition: every element in names contains a value*/
/*                 input by the user at the keyboard.     */

void printNames(const String names[], int lastIndex);
/* pre-condition:  each element in names is a NULL-        */
/*                 terminated sequence of characters.      */

void main(void)
{
  enum { lastIndex = 4, arraySize };
  String names[arraySize];

  getNames(names, lastIndex);
  printNames(names, lastIndex);
}
```

```
void getNames(String names[], int lastIndex)
{
  int i = 0;


  while (i <= lastIndex) {
    printf("Name? ");
    gets(names[i]);
    i++;
  }
}


void printNames(const String names[], int lastIndex)
{
  int i = 0;


  printf("The contents of the array are: \n");
  while (i <= lastIndex) {
    printf("%s \n", names[i]);
    i++;
  }
}
```

An example of a program run is

```
Name? Tom
Name? Dick
Name? Harry
Name? Ann
Name? May
The contents of the array are:
Tom
Dick
Harry
Ann
May
```

The problem with arrays of fixed length strings is that they use a lot of storage space; much of this space is wasted because we try to ensure that an array is large enough to contain any expected value. Since storage space is finite, we need a strategy for using only as much space as each individual string value needs. Let us see how this may be done.

First, we define a string type as a pointer to a *char*. (Remember that a pointer is a variable which stores an address.)

```
typedef char *String;
```

This allows us to define a variable of type *String* thus:

```
String name;
```

*name* is variable which is to contain the address of a single *char*. But we need to refer to a sequence of characters. So we define

```
char characterArray[BUFSIZ];
```

And then use *gets* as before to input the user-chosen string value.

```
printf("Name? ");
gets(characterArray);
```

Now we can determine how much storage is required for the value stored in *characterArray*.

```
storageRequired = (unsigned)strlen(characterArray) + 1;
```

(*+1* for the end of string character, '\0'). And then claim storage of just the right size to contain the contents of *characterArray* and place the start address of this store in *name*.

```
name = (String)malloc(storageRequired);
```

*malloc* allocates memory or storage. Here, it returns the address of a block of storage of size *storageRequired*. The cast operator (*String*) ensures that *malloc* returns storage suitable for values of type *String*.

Finally, we copy the contents of *characterArray* into the area pointed to by *name*.

```
strcpy(name, characterArray);
```

*strcpy* copies every character in *characterArray*, including the *NULL* character.

If the value stored in *characterArray* is *Tom\0* and *name* contains 65 (say), that is, the start address of the region which is large enough to contain the *Tom\0*, then we can imagine the picture to be thus

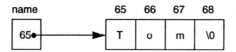

If we have an array of such pointers to strings

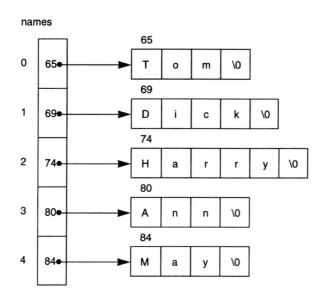

then we use only as much storage as is required. The address at which each string is stored is determined automatically by the C programming system via the memory allocation function, *malloc*. *malloc* is found in *stdlib*.

Here is the complete program.

```
/* program 6.7 - arrays of variable length strings. */

#include <stdio.h>
#include <stdlib.h>
#include <string.h>

typedef char *String;

void getNames(String names[], int lastIndex);
/* post-condition: every element in names contains a   */
/*                 NULL-terminated string value,        */
/*                 lastIndex is the highest element      */
/*                 number in names.                      */
```

```c
void printNames(const String names[], int lastIndex);
/* pre-condition:  every element in names contains a    */
/*                 NULL-terminated string value.         */


void main(void)
{
   enum { lastIndex = 4, arraySize = 5 };

   String names[arraySize];

   getNames(names, lastIndex);
   printNames(names, lastIndex);
}


void getNames(String names[], int lastIndex)
{
   char characterArray[BUFSIZ];
   String name;
   unsigned storageRequired;
   int i = 0;

   while (i <= lastIndex) {
     printf("Name? ");
     gets(characterArray);
    storageRequired = (unsigned)strlen(characterArray) + 1;
     name = (String)malloc(storageRequired);
     strcpy(name, characterArray);
     names[i] = name;
     i++;
   }
}

void printNames(const String names[], int lastIndex)
{
   int i = 0;

   while (i <= lastIndex) {
     printf("%s \n", names[i]);
     i++;
   }
}
```

## 6.9 Searching

Searching is the process of looking for an item. Common applications of searching include looking up the balance in a person's bank account, looking for a patient's hospital records and attempting to find the best candidate for a vacancy.

We illustrate the principles of the searching process by looking for a particular name in an array of names.

Suppose the array of names is

names

| Tom | Dick | Harry | Ann | May |
|-----|------|-------|-----|-----|
| 0 | 1 | 2 | 3 | 4 |

and the name we are looking for is *Harry*. Basically, we look at each name in the array in turn; if a name in the array matches the one we are looking for, then we terminate the search. If we get to the end of the array without having found a match, then we conclude the name we want is not in the array. Here is the function definition.

```
int nameIsInArray(const String name, const String names[],
                                            int lastIndex);
/* pre-condition:  names is initialised with pointers to */
/*                 NULL-terminated character sequences    */
/*                 lastIndex is the highest index of      */
/*                 array names                            */
/*                 name is a NULL-terminated value.       */
/* post-condition: returns 1 (ie TRUE) if name is in names,*/
/*                 otherwise, returns 0 (ie FALSE).       */
```

And here is the implementation.

```
int nameIsInArray(const String name, const String names[],
                                            int lastIndex)
{
   enum { false = 0, true = 1, identical = 0 };

   int i = 0;

   while (i <= lastIndex) {
     if (strcmp(names[i], name) == identical)
       return true;
     i++;
   }
   return false;
}
```

We look at the *i*th element in the array. (*i* can be any value from zero up to four in this example.) If we compare the *i*th element with the item we are looking for (*strcmp* compares strings and returns zero if they are identical) and find that they are identical, we return true (*name* is in *names*). However, if we reach the end of the array without returning, it is because *name* is not in *names*; we return false.

Here is a program which uses the search function.

```
/* program 6.8 - searches for a particular name in an */
/* array of names. */

#include <stdio.h>
#include <stdlib.h>
#include <string.h>

typedef char *String;

void buildNames(String names[]);
/* post-condition: returns an array in which each      */
/*                 element points to a NULL-terminated */
/*                 string value.                       */

int nameIsInArray(const String name,
                  const String names[], int lastIndex);
/* pre-condition:  every element in names is           */
/*                 initialised with a pointers to NULL- */
/*                 terminated character sequence        */
/*                 lastIndex is the highest index of   */
/*                 array names                         */
/*                 name is a NULL-terminate value.     */
/* post-condition: returns 1 (ie TRUE) if name is      */
/*                 in names,                           */
/*                 otherwise, returns 0 (ie FALSE).    */

String stringRead(char prompt[]);
/* post-condition: returns a pointer to a string */
/* entered at the keyboard. */

void main(void)
{
  enum { lastIndex = 4, arraySize = 5 };
  String names[arraySize];
  String name = stringRead("Search for which name? ");
  buildNames(names);
  if (nameIsInArray(name, names, lastIndex))
    printf("Found.\n");
  else
    printf("Name not found.\n");
}
```

```
void buildNames(String names[])
{
   names[0] = "Tom";
   names[1] = "Dick";
   names[2] = "Harry";
   names[3] = "Ann";
   names[4] = "May";
}


int nameIsInArray(const String name, const String names[],
                                          int lastIndex)

{
   enum { false = 0, true = 1, identical = 0 };

   int i = 0;

   while (i <= lastIndex) {
      if (strcmp(names[i], name) == identical)
         return true;
      i++;
   }
   return false;
}


String stringRead(char prompt[])
{
   char characterArray[BUFSIZ];
   unsigned storageRequired;
   String string;


   printf("%s", prompt);
   gets(characterArray);
   storageRequired = (unsigned)strlen(characterArray) + 1;
   string = (String)malloc(storageRequired);
   strcpy(string, characterArray);
   return string;
}
```

Three examples of program runs are

```
(1)   Search for which name? Tom
      Found.

(2)   Search for which name? May
      Found.

(3)   Search for which name? Mary
      Name not found.
```

Incidentally, the function *stringRead* is interesting. You remember that a function could only return a value of a fundamental type such as a *char*, *int* or *double*? Well, a function can also return an address. Since *String* is defined to be a pointer to a *char*, values of type *String* can be returned by a function. Hence the function prototype

```
String stringRead(char prompt[]);
```

is valid.

## 6.10  Sorting

Sorting is the process of placing items (such as people's names) into some kind of order (such as alphabetical order). We use an array of integers to illustrate the principles. We aim to sort the array shown below into ascending numerical order, namely 16  23  31  36  47.

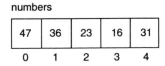

The location for the smallest value in numbers is zero; the value 47 is stored there. The smallest value is found in location 3. So we exchange the position of these two values.

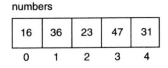

The location for the next smallest value is now one; the value 36 is stored there. We search from this position onwards for the next smallest value: it is 23 in location 2. We exchange the positions of these two values.

numbers

| 16 | 23 | 36 | 47 | 31 |
|----|----|----|----|----|
| 0  | 1  | 2  | 3  | 4  |

The location for the next smallest value is now two; the value 36 is stored there. We search from this position onwards for the next smallest value: it is 31 in location 4. We exchange the positions of these two values.

numbers

| 16 | 23 | 31 | 47 | 36 |
|----|----|----|----|----|
| 0  | 1  | 2  | 3  | 4  |

The location for the next smallest value is now three; the value 47 is stored there. We search from this position onwards for the next smallest value: it is 36 in location 4. We exchange the positions of these two values.

numbers

| 16 | 23 | 31 | 36 | 47 |
|----|----|----|----|----|
| 0  | 1  | 2  | 3  | 4  |

The contents of numbers are now in ascending numerical order. This sorting method, known as the insertion sorting algorithm, is used in the *sortIntArray* function shown below.

```
void sortIntArray(int numbers[], int lastIndex)
{
   int smallest;
   int locationContainingSmallest;
   int locationForNextSmallest = 0;

   while (locationForNextSmallest < lastIndex) {
      smallest = smallestInArray(numbers,
               locationForNextSmallest, lastIndex);
      locationContainingSmallest = locationOfSmallest(numbers,
                              smallest,
                              locationForNextSmallest,
                              lastIndex);
      swap(&numbers[locationForNextSmallest],
           &numbers[locationContainingSmallest]);
      locationForNextSmallest++;
   }
}
```

Program 6.9 shown below sorts an array of integers into ascending order.

```
/* program 6.9 - selection sort on an array of integers. */

#include <stdio.h>


void buildIntArray(int numbers[]);
/* post-condition: every element in numbers contain a value.*/


int locationOfSmallest(const int numbers[], int smallest,
                       int startIndex, int lastIndex);
/* pre-condition:   smallest is in numbers,                  */
/*                  startIndex <= lastIndex,                 */
/*                  lastIndex is highest index in numbers.*/
/* post-condition: returns location of smallest in          */
/*                  numbers.                                 */


int smallestInArray(const int numbers[], int startIndex,
                    int lastIndex);
/* pre-condition:   startIndex <= lastIndex,                 */
/*                  lastIndex is highest index in numbers.*/
/* post-condition: returns smallest value stored in         */
/*                  array between startIndex and            */
/*                  lastIndex inclusive.                    */


void sortIntArray(int numbers[], int lastIndex);
/* pre-condition:   lastIndex is the highest index in       */
/*                  numbers.                                 */
/* post-condition: items in numbers are in ascending        */
/*                  numerical order                         */

void swap(int *pX, int *pY);
/* post-condition: *pX' = *pY,                              */
/*                  *pY' = *pX                               */


void printIntArray(int numbers[], int lastIndex);
/* pre-condition:   lastIndex is the highest index in       */
/*                  numbers.                                 */
```

```
void main(void)
{
   enum { lastIndex = 4, arraySize };
   int numbers[arraySize];

   buildIntArray(numbers);
   sortIntArray(numbers, lastIndex);
   printIntArray(numbers, lastIndex);
}

void buildIntArray(int numbers[])
{
   numbers[0] = 47;
   numbers[1] = 36;
   numbers[2] = 23;
   numbers[3] = 16;
   numbers[4] = 31;
}

int locationOfSmallest(const int numbers[], int smallest,
                       int startIndex, int lastIndex)
{
   int i = startIndex;

   while (i <= lastIndex) {
     if (smallest == numbers[i])
       return i;
     i++;
   }
   return -1;  /* error */
}

int smallestInArray(const int numbers[], int startIndex,
                    int lastIndex)
{
   int i = startIndex;
   int smallest = numbers[i];

   while (i <= lastIndex) {
     if (numbers[i] < smallest)
       smallest = numbers[i];
     i++;
   }
 return smallest;
}
```

```
void sortIntArray(int numbers[], int lastIndex)
{
   int smallest;
   int locationContainingSmallest;
   int locationForNextSmallest = 0;

   while (locationForNextSmallest < lastIndex) {
     smallest = smallestInArray(numbers,
                 locationForNextSmallest, lastIndex);
     locationContainingSmallest = locationOfSmallest(numbers,
                                  smallest,
                                  locationForNextSmallest,
                                  lastIndex);
     swap(&numbers[locationForNextSmallest],
          &numbers[locationContainingSmallest]);
     locationForNextSmallest++;
   }
}


void swap(int *pX, int *pY)
{
   int hold = *pX;

   *pX = *pY;
   *pY = hold;
}


void printIntArray(int numbers[], int lastIndex)
{
   int i = 0;

   while (i <= lastIndex) {
     printf("%d  ", numbers[i]);
     i++;
   }
}
```

When run, this program displays

```
16    23    31    36    47
```

on the screen.

There are a few points to note. The specification for function *swap* is

```
void swap(int *pX, int *pY);
/* post-condition:  *pX' = *pY, */
/*                  *pY' = *pX  */
```

*pX* and *pY* contain the addresses of two different *int* variables. The post-condition

```
*pX' = *pY
```

says that, on exit from the function, the value stored at the address contained in *X* is the value stored at the address contained in *Y* on entry to the function.

The post-condition

```
*pY' = *pX
```

says that, on exit from the function, the value stored at the address contained in *Y* is the value stored at the address contained in *X* on entry to the function.

The effect of the function is to exchange the values stored in two variables. An example of a call to this function is

```
swap(&numbers[locationForNextSmallest],
                  &numbers[locationContainingSmallest]);
```

Here, the values stored in *numbers[locationForNextSmallest]* and *numbers[location-ContainingSmallest]* would be exchanged. The function's implementation is straightforward.

```
void swap(int *pX, int *pY)
{
   int hold = *pX;


   *pX = *pY;
   *pY = hold;
}
```

*hold* preserves the value stored in *\*pX* before it is overwritten with the value stored in *\*pY*.

The next point to note is the enumeration in main.

```
enum { lastIndex = 4, arraySize };
```

If an explicit value is not assigned to an enumeration constant, C automatically assigns the next number in sequence to it. So here, for example, C assigns the value 5 to *arraySize*. This is useful because if we were to change the size of the array, then we need only change one value – the value of *lastIndex*; C takes care of the *arraySize* for us.

## 6.11  Programming Principles

Do not refer to elements of an array which do not exist. For example, do not use an index value which is outside the bounds of an array. The bounds of an array are its first and last element numbers and the first element is always numbered zero.

Always ensure that any string values you create are terminated with the *NULL* character, otherwise, string handling functions may not perform as you expect them to. For example, *printf* may print garbage if you expect it print a sequence of characters that has not been properly terminated.

The first and last elements in an array represent its boundaries. Therefore, when devising test plans which involves searching through an array for example, remember to include as search values the values contained in the first and last elements.

Always initialise a pointer with an address.

*Exercise 6.3*

**1** Devise and test a function which will sort an array of string values into alphabetical order.

# 7

## Structures

### 7.1 Introduction

Let us suppose that a person's bank account contains the following details: their account number, their name and the balance left in their account. We can describe these attributes in a single structure.

```
typedef struct {
    String number;
    String name;
    double balance;
}   BankAccount;
```

Here, we have defined a *struct* type and named it *BankAccount*. *struct* is a C keyword. It introduces a structure declaration. The variables *name*, *number* and *balance* are the component parts of the structure named *BankAccount*. The component parts of a structure are known as members.

Since we have declared a type, we can define a variable to hold values of this type.

```
BankAccount bankAccount;
```

How can we place some values into this variable? We could write

```
bankAccount.number = "255386";
bankAccount.name = "Jones";
bankAccount.balance = 375.72;
```

So, to refer to a member of a particular structure, we use the form

*StructureName.MemberName*

We can display the contents of each member of a structure by using the dot member selector operator.

```
printf("%s %s %0.2f", bankAccount.accountNumber,
                    bankAccount.name, bankAccount.balance);
```

But the syntax is a little more complex when pointers to structures are involved, as we shall see.

Here is a program which fills a structure with a person's bank account details and then displays the details.

```
/* program 7.1 - a bank account structure. */

#include <stdio.h>
typedef char *String;

typedef struct {
  String number;
  String name;
  double balance;
} BankAccount;

BankAccount bankAccount(void);
/* post-condition: returns a bankAccount whose fields   */
/* contain values.                                       */

void printBankAccount(BankAccount *pBankAccount);

void main(void)
{
  BankAccount aBankAccount;

  aBankAccount = bankAccount();
  printBankAccount(&aBankAccount);
}

BankAccount bankAccount(void)
{
  BankAccount aBankAccount;

  aBankAccount.number = "147309";
  aBankAccount.name = "Marris";
  aBankAccount.balance = 150.0;
  return aBankAccount;
}
```

```
void printBankAccount(BankAccount *pBankAccount)
{
   printf("%s    %s    %0.2f", pBankAccount->number,
                               pBankAccount->name,
                               pBankAccount->balance);
}
```

The result of running this program is that

```
147309    Marris    150.00
```

is displayed on the screen.

The implementation of *bankAccount* is straightforward. It returns a structure with values assigned to each member.

In the function call

```
printBankAccount(&aBankAccount);
```

the address of the structure variable *aBankAccount* is passed to the pointer parameter *pBankAccount* in the function

```
void printBankAccount(BankAccount *pBankAccount)
```

The value stored in each member of the *bankAccount* structure is displayed by

```
printf("%s    %s    %0.2f", pBankAccount->number,
                            pBankAccount->name,
                            pBankAccount->balance);
```

Since *pBankAccount* contain the address of the structure, each member is selected by the –> operator.

So, if we have a pointer to a structure, we refer to a particular member by writing

*PointerToStructure->MemberName*

Whatever structure identifier we choose, the members are always referred to by the same name. For example, given the two variable definitions

```
BankAccount aBankAccount, anotherBankAccount;
```

we write

```
aBankAccount.number, aBankAccount.name,
aBankAccount.balance
```

and

```
anotherBankAccount.number, anotherBankAccount.name,
 anotherBankAccount.balance
```

A structure may be returned by a function. The address of a structure may be passed to a function parameter. And an entire structure can be passed as an argument value to a parameter – as shown below in another version of *printBankAccount*.

```
void printBankAccount(BankAccount bankAccount)
{
   printf("%s    %s    %0.2f", bankAccount.number,
                               bankAccount.name,
                               bankAccount.balance);

}
```

An example of a call to this function is

```
BankAccount bankAccount;
printBankAccount(bankAccount);
```

*BankAccount* is an example of a data structure sometimes known as a record. The component parts of a record are known as fields. However, in C, a record is known as a structure and a field is called a member.

## 7.2   Structure Arrays

A bank looks after many accounts. We can model a collection of accounts with an array in which each element is a structure.

```
BankAccount bankAccounts[5];
```

To refer to the *name* member of the *i*th element we would write

```
bankAccounts[i].name;
```

where *i* can be any value between 0 and 4 inclusive.
   Here is a program which shows how arrays of structures may be used.

```
/* program 7.2 - an array of bank records. */

#include <stdio.h>

typedef char *String;
```

```
typedef struct {
  String number;
  String name;
  double balance;
} BankAccount;

void buildScenario(BankAccount bankAccounts[]);
/* pre-condition: each element of bankAccounts contains */
/* a value.                                             */

void printAccounts(BankAccount bankAccounts[],
                                       int lastIndex);
/* pre-condition: lastIndex is the highest index       */
/* bankAccounts.                                        */

void main(void)
{
  enum { lastIndex = 4, arraySize };

  BankAccount bankAccounts[arraySize];

  buildScenario(bankAccounts);
  printAccounts(bankAccounts, lastIndex);
}

void buildScenario(BankAccount bankAccounts[])
{
  bankAccounts[0].number = "147309";
  bankAccounts[0].name = "Marris";
  bankAccounts[0].balance = 150.00;

  bankAccounts[1].number = "246890";
  bankAccounts[1].name = "Gupta";
  bankAccounts[1].balance = 255.00;

  bankAccounts[2].number = "135797";
  bankAccounts[2].name = "Green";
  bankAccounts[2].balance = -630.50;

  bankAccounts[3].number = "754811";
  bankAccounts[3].name = "Smith";
  bankAccounts[3].balance = 200.00;

  bankAccounts[4].number = "135797";
  bankAccounts[4].name = "Jones";
  bankAccounts[4].balance = 30.80;
}
```

```
void printAccounts(BankAccount bankAccounts[],
                                         int lastIndex)
{
  int i = 0;

  while (i <= lastIndex) {
    printf("%s    %s    £%0.2f\n", bankAccounts[i].number,
         bankAccounts[i].name, bankAccounts[i].balance);
    i++;
  }
}
```

The output from this program is

```
147309    Marris    £150.00
246890    Gupta     £255.00;
135797    Green     £-630.50;
754811    Smith     £200.00;
135797    Jones     £30.80;
```

This time, it is an array which is passed as an argument value to both *buildScenario* and *printAccounts*. So the . (dot) operator is used in both functions to select a member.

*Exercise 7.1*

**1** From time to time the current balance in a particular account is required. Design a function which, if given an account number, returns the balance in the account with that number – if it exists. A specification for this function could be

```
double balanceInAccount(const BankAccount bankAccounts[],
                  int lastIndex, String accountNumber);
/* pre-condition: lastIndex is the highest index in   */
/* bankAccounts.                                       */
/* bankAccounts. accountNumber is in bankAccounts.     */
/* post-condition: returns balance in account for which*/
/* bankAccounts[i].number == accountNumber.            */
```

However, since you cannot retrieve a balance from a bank account which does not exist, you should also provide a function which returns true if there is an account for a given account number, false otherwise.

Include the functions in program 7.2 shown above and, after making suitable amendments to main, test them.
**2** The balance in most accounts does not stay the same for long; withdrawals are made to pay for goods and services and from time to time deposits are made to increase the balance. Design, write and test a function, which if given an account

number and a transaction updates the balance held in the account for the given account number.

3  A direct computer supplies mail order business maintains a price list of computer hardware it offers for sale. An entry in the price list contains

a catalogue code  –  a six-character number, e.g. MAR299
an item name     –  e.g. Marris Magic Printer
a description    –  e.g. 24-pin dot matrix printer
a price          –  e.g. £99.99

(a)  Design a suitable data structure to contain about seven entries in the price list.
(b)  State the specification for a function which will "build the scenario", that is, which will fill the data structure you designed in (a) with sample test data. Then write the function implementation.
(c)  State the specification for a function which will display the entire price list. Then write and test the function.
(d)  Every price in the list is to be increased by, say, 10%. State the specification for a function which will return the required percentage increase input by the person running the program. Then write the function.
(e)  Write the specification for a function which will increase every price in the price list by the percentage increase entered by the user; the percentage increase value must be a parameter to the function. Then write and test the function.

4  An airline maintains a record of the seats available on each of its scheduled flights. The following information is recorded.

flight number
maximum number of seats available
number of seats currently booked

Design, write and test a C program which will simulate the booking activities of the airline. When a reservation is made, the number of seats currently booked is increased by the requested number of seats but only if there are enough seats available. When a cancellation is made, then the number of seats booked is decreased.

## 7.3  Member Arrays

A small leisure centre has a single squash court. Owing to the popularity of the court during Monday and Friday lunchtimes, a booking system is used for these times. Members may book the court up to six days in advance.

To help us to appreciate the situation, let us look at an example of a booking process dialogue between a member and the receptionist.

Member: I would like to book a squash court.
Receptionist: Certainly. Which day?

Member: Monday please.
Receptionist consults the bookings made so far.
Receptionist: The court is free at 12 and at 1 pm on that day.
Member: What about 2?
Receptionist: Sorry. The court is booked at 2. Would you like another time or another day?
Member: What about Friday?
Receptionist consults bookings made so far.
Receptionist: The court is free at 2 pm on Friday.
Member: That will suit me very nicely.
Receptionist: Which name please?
Member: Smith
Receptionist: The court is now booked for you.
Member: Thank you.

We can model the bookings diary as an array in which each element is a structure or record, one for each array index or time slot.

| Array Index | Day | Time | Name |
|---|---|---|---|
| 0 | Mon | 12 | |
| 1 | Mon | 1 | |
| 2 | Mon | 2 | Patel |
| 3 | Fri | 12 | Jones |
| 4 | Fri | 1 | French |
| 5 | Fri | 2 | Smith |

The court is free on Monday at 12 and at 1 pm, but is booked at all other times. The bookings data structure is easily defined in C.

First, we define the structure of one booking, that is, one entry in the bookings diary.

```
typedef struct {
    String day;
    unsigned time;
    String name;
}  BookingEntry;
```

But the diary is made up of several such entries.

```
typedef struct {
  int lastIndex;
  BookingEntry bookingsArray[6];
} BookingsDiary;
```

Here, we have combined the array and its last index value into a single structure named *BookingsDiary*. Why? Suppose, for example, we want to display the entire contents of the bookings diary. Two possible calls to a function to perform this task are

```
(1)    showAllBookings(bookingsDiary, lastIndex);
```

and

```
(2)    showAllBookings(bookingsDiary);
```

In the first example, we pass an array together with its last index value. In the second example, we pass a structure which contains the array together with its last index. The second example is preferred because it has fewer arguments than the first example. However, *lastIndex* must be initialised with a value. This can be done in the function which sets up the initial contents of the bookings diary.

```
BookingsDiary emptyBookings(void)
{

   BookingsDiary bookings;

   bookings.bookingsArray[0].day = "Mon";
   bookings.bookingsArray[0].time = 12u;
   bookings.bookingsArray[0].name = blank;

   bookings.bookingsArray[1].day = "Mon";
   bookings.bookingsArray[1].time = 1u;
   bookings.bookingsArray[1].name = blank;
   bookings.bookingsArray[2].day = "Mon";

   . . .

   bookings.bookingsArray[5].time = 2u;
   bookings.bookingsArray[5].name = blank;

   bookings.lastIndex = 5;
   return bookings;
}
```

*blank* is defined to be the space character " ". Since we need to use *blank* in various functions throughout the program, we write

```
#define blank " "
```

near the top of the program just before the implementation of the first function (*main* in our case). In the compiler's pre-translation stage, every occurrence of the word *blank* in a statement is replaced with " " (that is, quotes space quotes). So, for example, the pre-processor part of the compiler replaces

```
bookings.bookingsArray[5].name = blank;
```

with

```
bookings.bookingsArray[5].name = " ";
```

The substitution of *blank* with " " does not occur inside comments such as

```
/* blank out the name. */
```

or within quoted strings such as

```
printf("Replace blank with quotes-space-quotes");
```

Notice that there is no space between *#* and *define* and the line is not terminated with a semi-colon. *#define* is an example of a pre-processor directive.

The user's view of the program is a menu which provides the following operations

1 make a booking
2 show all bookings
3 at the end of the day, clear the day's bookings.

The programmer's view of the program is shown in the structure chart – see Figure 7.1.

The specifications of the main functions are

```
BookingEntry aBooking(String day, unsigned time, String
                                                    name);
```

```
/* post-condition:  returns a booking assembled from    */
/*                   day, time and name.                 */
```

```
BookingsDiary bookingsAfterBookingMade(BookingsDiary
                                                 bookings);
```

```
/* post-condition:  returns bookings with (possibly)    */
/*                   a new booking included.             */
```

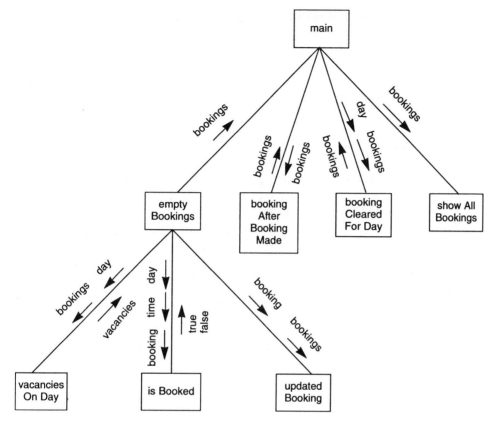

**Figure 7.1** Structure chart for program 7.3 – squash court reservations.

```
BookingsDiary bookingsClearedForDay(BookingsDiary
                                bookings, String day);

/* post-condition:  returns bookings with all names  */
/*                   for day blanked.                 */

BookingsDiary emptyBookings(void);
/* post-condition: every name in bookings is blank.   */

int isBooked(BookingsDiary bookings, unsigned time,
                                    String day);
/* post-condition:  returns true if name for day and  */
/*                   time is not blank                 */
/*                   otherwise returns false.          */
```

```
void showAllBookings(BookingsDiary bookings);
/* prints the entire bookings diary. */

BookingsDiary updatedBookings(BookingsDiary bookings,
                                    BookingEntry booking);
/* post-condition:   returns bookings with booking    */
/*                   included.                         */



unsigned vacanciesOnDay(BookingsDiary bookings,
                                    String day);
/* post-condition:   returns the number of vacant,    */
/*                   unbooked slots on day.            */
```

The main function makes calls to *emptyBookings*, *bookingsAfterBookingMade*, *showAllBookings* and *bookingsClearedForDay*.

```
void main(void)
{
  enum { false = 0, true };

  BookingsDiary bookings;
  BookingEntry aBooking;
  String reply, day;
  int done = false;

  bookings = emptyBookings();
  while (!done) {
    reply = stringRead(
        "\nBookings menu: (M)ake, (S)how, (C)lear, (Q)uit: ");
    reply[0] = toupper(reply[0]);
    switch (reply[0]) {
    case 'M':
      bookings = bookingsAfterBookingMade(bookings);
      break;
    case 'S':
      showAllBookings(bookings);
      break;
    case 'C':
      day = dayRead();
      bookings = bookingsClearedForDay(bookings, day);
      break;
```

```
    case 'Q':
      done = true;
      break;
    default: /* unexpected value in reply[0]. */
      break;
    }
  }
}
```

Here we have used a simple menu; the user is invited to enter the first letter of their choice. This is stored in *reply*. Then, we used a new control structure, the *switch* or *case* construct, to process the user's choice.

The *switch* construct functions in a way similar to, but different from, a sequence of *else ifs*.

```
if (reply[0] == 'M')
  bookings = bookingsAfterBookingMade(bookings);
else if (reply[0] == 'S')
  showAllBookings(bookings);
else if (reply[0] == 'C') {
  day = dayRead();
  bookings = bookingsClearedForDay(bookings, day);
}
else if (reply[0] ==  'Q')
  done = true;
else
  /* unexpected character in reply[0]. */
```

The *switch* statement selects a *case* for execution. The *case* selected depends on the value contained in *reply[0]*. So, for example, if *reply[0]* contains 'S' then

```
case 'S':
  showAllBookings(bookings);
  break;
```

is executed.

The *break* statement prevents the cases which follow *case 'S'*: from being executed. The *default* case in the switch construction corresponds in its function to the trailing else clause in a sequence of *else ifs*; it caters for none of the preceding cases. The default case is optional just as the trailing else is optional. The *return* statement is also used to prevent fall through to the next case, as shown below in the *bookingsAfterBookingsMade* function.

```
BookingsDiary bookingsAfterBookingMade(BookingsDiary
                                              bookings)
{
  enum { false, true, identical = 0 };


  typedef enum { day, time, name } State;


  String aDay, aName;
  unsigned aTime;
  BookingEntry aNewBooking;
  unsigned vacancies;
  State state = day;


  while (true) {
    switch(state) {
    case day:
      aDay = dayRead();
      if (strcmp(aDay, "None") == identical)
        return bookings;
      vacancies = vacanciesOnDay(bookings, aDay);
      if (vacancies == 0u)
        state = day;
      else
        state = time;
      break;


    case time:
      aTime = timeRead();
      if (aTime == 0u)
        return bookings;
      if (isBooked(bookings, aTime, aDay)) {
        printf(
              "\nThe time is booked - choose another.\n");
        state = time;
      }
      else
        state = name;
      break;
```

```
    case name:
      aName = nameRead();
      aNewBooking = aBooking(aDay, aTime, aName);
      bookings = updatedBookings(bookings, aNewBooking);
      if (isBooked(bookings, aTime, aDay))
        printf("Booking confirmed\n");
      else
        printf("Error in booking.\n");
      return bookings;
    }
  }
}
```

The implementation of *bookingsAfterBookingMade* is a little tricky because the steps involved in making a booking are not necessarily the same for every booking made. We need to reflect the receptionist's way of working. First, we recognise that there are three different situations or states; these are defined in the *enum*

```
typedef enum { day, time, name } State;
```

(In the absence of specific values, the compiler automatically assigns zero to *day*, one to *time* and two to *name*.)

In the *day* state we establish the day required by the member and offer an alternative day if needed. We remain in the *day* state until either a day is chosen, or no days are chosen. If no days are chosen (that is, *None*) then we exit from the function via the *return* statement. If a day is chosen, then we pass onto the *time* state.

We remain in the *time* state if the chosen day and time are already booked; we offer an alternative time. If there is no time slot available, then we exit from the function via the *return* statement. If an agreeable time slot has been found, then we pass on to the *name* state.

We remain in the *name* state just to obtain the member's name and to make and confirm the booking. Then we exit from the function via the *return* statement.

Now, the expression

```
while (true) {
   ...
}
```

means loop for ever. But we break out of the loop by exiting (that is, returning) from the function at appropriate times.

Here is an incomplete version of the program.

```
/* part of program 7.3 - squash court reservation system   */

#include <stdio.h>
#include <stdlib.h>
#include <string.h>
#include <ctype.h>

typedef char *String;


typedef struct {
    String day;
    unsigned time;
    String name;
}   BookingEntry;


typedef struct {
  int lastIndex;
  BookingEntry bookingsArray[6];
} BookingsDiary;


BookingEntry aBooking(String day, unsigned time,
                                         String name);
/* post-condition: returns a booking assembled from   */
/*                 day, time and name.                 */


BookingsDiary bookingsAfterBookingMade(
                        BookingsDiary bookings);
/* post-condition: returns bookings with (possibly)    */
/*                 a new booking included.             */


BookingsDiary bookingsClearedForDay(BookingsDiary
                             bookings, String day);
/* post-condition: returns bookings with all bookings  */
/* :               for day blanked.                    */

String dayRead(void);
/* post-condition: returns either Mon or Fri or None.  */

BookingsDiary emptyBookings(void);
/* post-condition: every booking is blank.             */
```

```
int isBooked(BookingsDiary bookings, unsigned time,
                                         String day);
/* post-condition: returns true if name for day and time*/
/*                 is blank, otherwise returns false    */



String nameRead(void);
/* post-condition: returns name entered at the keyboard.*/



void showAllBookings(BookingsDiary bookings);
/* prints the entire bookings schedule.                 */

String stringRead(char prompt[]);
/* post-condition: returns string entered at the        */
/*                 keyboard.                             */



unsigned timeRead(void);
/* post-condition: returns booking time input at the    */
/*                 either 0 or 12 or 1 or 2              */



unsigned unsignedNumberRead(char prompt[]);
/* post-condition: returns number entered at keyboard.  */



BookingsDiary updatedBookings(BookingsDiary bookings,
                                 BookingEntry booking);
/* post-condition: returns bookings with booking        */
/*                 included.                             */


unsigned vacanciesOnDay(BookingsDiary bookings,
                                         String day);
/* post-condition: returns the number of vacant,        */
/*                 unbooked slots on day.                */


#define blank " "
```

```
void main(void)
{
  enum { false = 0, true };

  BookingsDiary bookings;
  BookingEntry aBooking;
  String reply, day;
  int done = false;

  bookings = emptyBookings();
  while (!done) {
    reply = stringRead(
        "\nBookings menu: (M)ake, (S)how, (C)lear, (Q)uit: ");
    reply[0] = toupper(reply[0]);
    switch (reply[0]) {
    case 'M':
      bookings = bookingsAfterBookingMade(bookings);
      break;
    case 'S':
      showAllBookings(bookings);
      break;
    case 'C':
      day = dayRead();
      bookings = bookingsClearedForDay(bookings, day);
      break;
    case 'Q':
      done = true;
      break;
      }
    }
}


BookingEntry aBooking(String day, unsigned time,
                                              String name)
{
  BookingEntry booking;

  booking.day = day;
  booking.time = time;
  booking.name = name;
  return booking;
}
```

```
BookingsDiary bookingsAfterBookingMade(BookingsDiary bookings)
{
  enum { false, true, identical = 0 };


  typedef enum { day, time, name } State;


  String aDay, aName;
  unsigned aTime;
  BookingEntry aNewBooking;
  unsigned vacancies;
  State state = day;


  while (true) {
    switch(state) {


    case day:
      aDay = dayRead();
      if (strcmp(aDay, "None") == identical)
        return bookings;
      vacancies = vacanciesOnDay(bookings, aDay);
      if (vacancies == 0u)
        state = day;
      else
        state = time;
      break;


    case time:
      aTime = timeRead();
      if (aTime == 0u)
        return bookings;
      if (isBooked(bookings, aTime, aDay)) {
        printf(
             "\nThe time is booked - choose another.\n");
        state = time;
      }
      else
        state = name;
      break;
```

```
    case name:
      aName = nameRead();
      aNewBooking = aBooking(aDay, aTime, aName);
      bookings = updatedBookings(bookings, aNewBooking);
      if (isBooked(bookings, aTime, aDay))
        printf("Booking confirmed\n");
      else
        printf("Error in booking.\n");
      return bookings;
    }
  }
}



BookingsDiary bookingsClearedForDay(BookingsDiary
                                    bookings, String theDay)
{
  enum { identical = 0 };

  int i = 0;

  while (i <= bookings.lastIndex) {
  if (strcmp(bookings.bookingsArray[i].day, theDay) ==
  identical)
    bookings.bookingsArray[i].name = blank;
    i++;
  }
  return bookings;
}

String dayRead(void)
{
  String day = stringRead("\nDay (Mon or Fri or None)? ");

  while ((strcmp(day, "Mon") != 0u) &&
         (strcmp(day, "Fri") != 0u) &&
         (strcmp(day, "None") != 0u)) {
    printf("\nDay chosen is not available.\n");
    day = stringRead("\nDay (Mon or Fri or None)? ");
  }
  return day;
}
```

```
BookingsDiary emptyBookings(void)
{
    BookingsDiary bookings;

    bookings.bookingsArray[0].day = "Mon";
    bookings.bookingsArray[0].time = 12u;
    bookings.bookingsArray[0].name = blank;
    bookings.bookingsArray[1].day = "Mon";
    bookings.bookingsArray[1].time = 1u;
    bookings.bookingsArray[1].name = blank;
    bookings.bookingsArray[2].day = "Mon";
    bookings.bookingsArray[2].time = 2u;
    bookings.bookingsArray[2].name = blank;
    bookings.bookingsArray[3].day = "Fri";
    bookings.bookingsArray[3].time = 12u;
    bookings.bookingsArray[3].name = blank;
    bookings.bookingsArray[4].day = "Fri";
    bookings.bookingsArray[4].time = 1u;
    bookings.bookingsArray[4].name = blank;
    bookings.bookingsArray[5].day = "Fri";
    bookings.bookingsArray[5].time = 2u;
    bookings.bookingsArray[5].name = blank;
    bookings.lastIndex = 5;
    return bookings;
}


int isBooked(BookingsDiary bookings, unsigned theTime,
                                        String theDay)
{
    return 0;
}


String nameRead(void)
{
    return stringRead("\nName? ");
}
```

```
void showAllBookings(BookingsDiary bookings)
{
}

String stringRead(char prompt[])
{
  char charArray[BUFSIZ];
  String string;

  unsigned storageRequired;

  printf("%s", prompt);
  gets(charArray);
  storageRequired = (unsigned)strlen(charArray) + 1;
  string = (String)malloc(storageRequired);
  strcpy(string, charArray);
  return string;
}
unsigned timeRead(void)
{
  return 0u;
}

unsigned unsignedNumberRead(char prompt[])
{
  char charArray[BUFSIZ];
  unsigned number = 0u;

  printf("%s", prompt);
  gets(charArray);
  sscanf(charArray, "%u", &number);
  return number;
}

BookingsDiary updatedBookings(BookingsDiary bookings,
                              BookingEntry booking)
{
  return bookings;
}

unsigned vacanciesOnDay(BookingsDiary bookings,
                                        String theDay)
{
  return 0u;
}
```

An example of a program run is:

```
Bookings menu: (M)ake, (S)how, (C)lear, (Q)uit: M

Day (Mon, Fri or None)? Mon

Current bookings for Mon are:

Mon 12
Mon  1
Mon  2 Jones

Time (12, 1, 2, or 0)?  0

Bookings menu: (M)ake, (S)how, (C)lear, (Q)uit: M

Day (Mon, Fri or None)? Fri

Current bookings for Fri are:

Fri 12 French
Fri  1 Kline
Fri  2

Time (12, 1, 2 or 0)? 2

Name? Smith

Current bookings for Fri are:

Fri 12 French
Fri  1 Kline
Fri  2

Bookings menu: (M)ake, (S)how, (C)lear, (Q)uit: Q
```

## Exercise 7.2

1 Complete and test the functions isBooked, showAllBookings, timeRead, updatedBookings and vacanciesOnDay as defined in program 7.3 above.
2 The small leisure centre described in section 7.3 now has two squash courts. Amend program 7.3 so that

    (a) bookings are maintained for two courts and
    (b) bookings may also be made for Wednesdays at 12, 1 and 2pm.

# 8

## Files

### 8.1  Files, Records and Fields

Every year The City holds a marathon. Runners apply to enter the competition by filling in a form and sending it, together with the fee, to the organiser. The organiser of The City marathon maintains a computer file of all registered competitors. Part of the information recorded for each competitor is

name
age
gender

Part of the file might look like

| Name | Age | Gender | |
|------|-----|--------|--|
| Cartwright | 29 | f | |
| Jones | 45 | m | |
| Stevenson | 51 | m | ← a record |
| Patel | 29 | f | |
| | ↑ | | |
| | age | | |
| | field | | |

Each attribute (name, age, gender) is an example of a field. The different fields together make up a single structure known as a record. In our example there is one record for each competitor. A file contains many records.

We can model the record in C as a fixed-length structure like this

```
typedef struct {
  char name[BUFSIZ];
  int age;
  char gender;
} CompetitorStructure;
```

The length or size of the structure is returned by the C *sizeof* function.

```
unsigned structureSize =
                  (unsigned)sizeof(CompetitorStructure);
```

## 8.2  File Creation

To place records in a new file we

*define file and record variables*
*open the file*
*while not finished*
  *assemble a record from its field values*
  *write the record to the file*
*endwhile*
*close the file*

So, to place competitor records (defined in section 8.1 above) on a new competitors file we write

```
void main(void)
{
   CompetitorStructure competitorRecord;
   FILE *competitorsFile = fopen("compet.dat", "wb");

   readCharArray("\nName (* to finish)? ",
                                 competitorRecord.name);
   while (competitorRecord.name[0] != '*') {
     competitorRecord.age = intNumberRead("Age? ");
     competitorRecord.gender = charRead("Gender (m/f)? ");

     fwrite(&competitorRecord,
             sizeof(CompetitorStructure),1,competitorsFile);

     readCharArray("\nName (* to finish)? ",
                                 competitorRecord.name);
   }
   fclose(competitorsFile);
}
```

*CompetitorStructure* is the record structure defined in section 8.1 above. The line

```
FILE *competitorsFile = fopen("compet.dat", "wb");
```

• defines a variable of type (pointer to) *FILE* named *competitorsFile*

- declares that the file is to be saved on disk under the name *compet.dat*
- opens a new file ready for writing binary data to it
- overwrites any existing file with the name *compet.dat.*

*fopen* makes a connection between the variable file name used inside the program (*competitorsFile*) and the external file name used outside the program by the computer's operating system (*compet.dat*). The file open mode, *wb*, destroys any existing file with the name *compet.dat*. *wb* stands for write binary mode.
    The function call

```
readCharArray("\nName (* to finish)? ",
                                competitorRecord.name);
```

displays the prompt *Name (* to finish)?* on the screen and stores the user's response in the name field of *competitorRecord*.
    We loop for as long as the first character stored in *competitorRecord.name* is not *. In the loop we fill the remaining fields with values, write the record to the file and ask for the next name to be input.
    The statement

```
fwrite(&competitorRecord, sizeof(CompetitorStructure), 1,
                                competitorsFile);
```

says write a copy of the data held in a competitors record into the competitors file. The arguments *sizeof(CompetitorStructure)* and *1* mean one item of size equal to the record structure.
    Records are written onto the file sequentially, one record after another.

```
Cartwright 29 f   Jones 45 m Stevenson 51 m   Patel 29 f
```

Notice the repeating pattern in types of the data held:

```
array-of-char int char array-of-char int char ...
```

(The fact that data are converted into binary format before being written to the file need not concern us here.) Finally, we close the file.

```
fclose(competitorsFile);
```

*fclose* breaks the connection between the variable file name *competitorsFile* and the external file name *compet.dat*; it also ensures that the last bit of data is physically written into the file.
    *FILE*, *fopen*, *wb* and *fclose* are all defined in *stdio*.

## 8.3   Record Retrieval

To display the contents of a file we

*define file and record variables*
*open the file*
*retrieve the first record from the file*
*while the end of the file has not been reached*
  *display the contents of each field in the record*
  *retrieve the next record from the file*
*endwhile*
*close the file*

To display the contents of the competitors file we write

```
void main(void)
{
   CompetitorStructure competitorRecord;
   FILE *competitorsFile = fopen("compet.dat", "rb");

   fread(&competitorRecord, sizeof(CompetitorStructure),
                                    1, competitorsFile);
   while (!feof(competitorsFile)) {
      printf("%s   ", competitorRecord.name);
      printf("%d   ", competitorRecord.age);
      printf("%c   ", competitorRecord.gender);
      fread(&competitorRecord, sizeof(CompetitorStructure),
                                    1, competitorsFile);
   }
   fclose(competitorsFile);
}
```

The line

```
FILE *competitorsFile = fopen("compet.dat", "rb");
```

- defines a variable of type (pointer to) *FILE* named *competitorsFile*
- declares that the file to be opened is named *compet.dat* on disk
- opens an existing file ready for retrieving binary data from it.

The argument *rb* stands for read binary mode.
  The statement

```
fread(&competitorRecord, sizeof(CompetitorStructure), 1,
                                    competitorsFile);
```

says read a record from the *competitorsFile* and place a copy of it in *competitorRecord*. The arguments *sizeof(CompetitorStructure)* and *1* mean one item of size equal to the record structure. Suppose the file was created thus

```
Cartwright 29 f   Jones 45 m  Stevenson 51 m   Patel 29 f
```

then, when the first record is read, Cartwright would be placed in the name field, 29 in the age field and f in the gender field.

If the end of the file has been reached and there are no more records to be read, then *fread* fails to retrieve a record and *feof* (for end of file) is set to *TRUE*. So we write

```
while (!feof(competitorsFile)) {
    ...
}
```

## 8.4   Shared File and Record Declarations

A record retrieval program will fail if

• there is no file on disk to open and retrieve data from
• the record structure used in the file creation program is different from the record structure used in the record retrieval program.

For example, if the file was created with the following record structure

```
array-of-char int char
```

then retrieving a record from the file and placing it in record variable of the form

```
int array-of-char char
```

is a recipe for creating garbage. (You try fitting an array of characters into a single *int* variable.) Therefore it would be sensible if both file creation and record retrieval programs shared the same copy of the external file name and record structure. So we create a copy of these declarations, using our usual program editor, and save it with the name *compet.h* (say). This is what *compet.h* looks like.

```
/* compet.h - contains competitor file record structure */
/*            and external file name.                    */


#include <stdio.h>

#define diskFileName "compet.dat"
```

```
typedef struct {
  char name[BUFSIZ];
  int age;
  char gender;
} CompetitorStructure;
```

We do not compile or run *compet.h*, but we *#include* it in our programs as shown below.

```
/* program 8.1 - sets up a Marathon File with competitors. */

#include <stdio.h>
#include <string.h>

#include "compet.h"

char charRead(char prompt[]);
/* post-condition: returns a char entered at the keyboard. */

int intNumberRead(char prompt[]);
/* post-condition: returns a number entered at the keyboard. */

void readCharArray(char prompt[], char array[]);
/* post-condition: array' contains a string entered at  */
/* the keyboard.                                         */

void main(void)
{
  CompetitorStructure competitorRecord;
  FILE *competitorsFile = fopen(competitorDiskFileName, "wb");

  printf("File creation program.\n");
  readCharArray("\nName (* to finish)? ",
                                   competitorRecord.name);
  while (competitorRecord.name[0] != '*') {
    competitorRecord.age = intNumberRead("Age? ");
    competitorRecord.gender = charRead("Gender (m/f)? ");
    fwrite(&competitorRecord, sizeof(CompetitorStructure),
                                   1, competitorsFile);
    readCharArray("\nName (* to finish)? ",
                                   competitorRecord.name);
  }
  fclose(competitorsFile);
  printf("\nFinished.\n");
}
```

```
char charRead(char prompt[])
{
  char charArray[BUFSIZ];

  printf("%s", prompt);
  gets(charArray);
  return charArray[0];
}


int intNumberRead(char prompt[])
{
  char charArray[BUFSIZ];
  int number = 0;

  printf("%s", prompt);
  gets(charArray);
  sscanf(charArray, "%d", &number);
  return number;
}


void readCharArray(char prompt[], char charArray[])
{
  printf("%s", prompt);
  gets(charArray);
}
```

An example of a program run is

```
File creation program.

Name (* to finish)? Cartwright
Age? 29
Gender (m/f)? f

Name (* to finish)? Jones
Age? 45
Gender (m/f)? m

Name (* to finish)? *

Finished.
```

At compile time, the line *#include "compet.h"* is replaced with the contents of *compet.h*. Notice the use of quotation marks rather than angle brackets to delimit the name of the text for inclusion; usually, the quotation marks mean that the text to be included is found in the same place as the program source text. When the contents of an included text file is changed, then all the programs that *#include* the text file must be re-compiled.

Any named collection of data which is stored on disk is known as a file. So program source text and headers are referred to as files. An executable program held on disk is also known as a file. And a file is also a collection of records.

Now we address the problem of attempting to read from a file which does not exist. Fortunately, if a file cannot be opened, *fopen* returns *NULL*. So we can write

```
FILE *competitorsFile = fopen(competitorDiskFileName, "rb");

if (competitorsFile == NULL) {
  printf("\nProgram halted: unable to open %s\n",
                            competitorDiskFileName);
  exit(EXIT_FAILURE);
}
```

*exit* is a C keyword. It halts program execution, flushing buffers and closing files as it does so. Both *exit* and *EXIT_FAILURE* are defined in *stdlib. exit* and *EXIT_FAILURE* are used in program 8.2 shown below.

```
/* program 8.2 - Displays contents of Marathon Entries */
/*                File.                                 */


#include <stdio.h>
#include <stdlib.h>
#include "compet.h"


void main(void)
{
  FILE *competitorsFile;
  CompetitorStructure competitorRecord;

  competitorsFile = fopen(competitorDiskFileName, "rb");
  if (competitorsFile == NULL) {
    printf("Program halted: unable to open %s.\n",
                                competitorDiskFileName);
    exit(EXIT_FAILURE);
  }
  fread(&competitorRecord, sizeof(CompetitorStructure),
                                1, competitorsFile);
```

```
    while (!feof(competitorsFile)) {
      printf("%s   ", competitorRecord.name);
      printf("%d   ", competitorRecord.age);
      printf("%c   ", competitorRecord.gender);
      printf("\n");
      fread(&competitorRecord, sizeof(CompetitorStructure),
                                    1, competitorsFile);
    }
    fclose(competitorsFile);
}
```

A result of running program 8.2 is that

```
Cartwright   29   f
Jones   45   m
Stevenson   51   m
Patel   29   f
```

is shown on the screen. The appearance would be improved if we could arrange the output in columns thus

```
Cartwright     29   f
Jones          45   m
Stevenson      51   m
Patel          29   f
```

This can be done if we specify a space on the screen in which the contents of a field is to be displayed. For example, the statement

```
printf("%-12s   ", competitorRecord.name);
```

says print the contents of *competitorRecord.name* left justified in a space 12 characters wide. For example

Space taken up by 12 characters

Similarly,

```
printf("%4d", competitorRecord.age);
```

says print the contents of *competitorRecord.age* right justified in a space four characters wide.

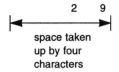

space taken
up by four
characters

And

```
printf("%3c", competitorRecord.gender);
```

says print the contents of *competitorRecord.gender* right justified in a space three characters wide.

The space allocated for printing a value is known as the field width. A signed integer preceding the conversion specification character is known as the field width specifier. A minus sign indicates left justified; no sign or a plus sign indicates right justified. So, for example: *"%-10s"* means display a string value left justified in a field width of 10 and *"%10s"* means display a string value right justified in a field width of 10.

## 8.5   Data Dictionaries

We specify the file content and record structure in a data dictionary. See Figure 8.1 for example.

The data store name is the name of the file on disk. The description is a general description of the file, its content and purpose. Under Data Name we list the file, structure and member variable names, and, under the Type heading, their types. The comments column includes explanations of the various entries.

**DATA DICTIONARY**

| **Author** | Terry Marris | | **Date**   8 May 1995 |
|---|---|---|---|

**Data Store name**   compet.dat

**Description**       file of competitor records

| **Data Name** | **Type** | **Comments** |
|---|---|---|
| competitorFile | FILE | File of competitor records |
| competitor | CompetitorStructure | one per competitor |
|   name | array of char | |
|   age | int | |
|   gender | char | values 'm' or 'f' |

**Figure 8.1**   Data dictionary specifying the competitor file structure and content.

*Exercise 8.1*

**Remember to use data dictionaries to specify your records and files.**

1 The local constabulary wishes to create a register of bicycles and their owners as part of their efforts to detect and deter theft and to return recovered cycles. The data to be recorded include owner's name, date of birth, post code, house number, bicycle frame number and bicycle frame type (for example, diamond, open or tandem). Write and test two programs, one to create the register (that is, file) with about seven records, and one to display the contents of the file neatly in columns; each column should have its own heading.

2 A network manager maintains a central file of the software packages used within a college. The data recorded for each package include its name, type (word processor, spreadsheet, database or compiler, for example), licence number, number of licensed copies and locations installed. Write and test two programs, one to create the file and one to display its contents in tabular format (that is, in a table).

## 8.6   File to Printer

We need to print out the contents of the marathon entries file; copies are needed for the organiser (so that all the entry details may be checked), for the finish marshals (so that they can produce the results of the race) and for the commentator (so that runners of note may be identified). Program 8.3 displays the contents of the marathon entries file on the printer.

```
/* program 8.3 - Displays contents of Marathon Entries File */
/*               on the printer.                          */


#include <stdio.h>
#include <stdlib.h>
#include "compet.h"
#define printerDevice  "LPT1"


void main(void)
{
   FILE *printer = fopen(printerDevice, "w");
   FILE *competitorsFile = fopen(competitorDiskFileName, "rb");
   CompetitorStructure competitorRecord;
```

```
   if (printer == NULL) {
     printf(
            "Program halted: unable to access printer\n.");
     exit(EXIT_FAILURE);
   }
   if (competitorsFile == NULL) {
     printf("Program halted: unable to open %s.\n",
                                    competitorDiskFileName);
     exit(EXIT_FAILURE);
   }
   fread(&competitorRecord,sizeof(CompetitorStructure),1,
                                          competitorsFile);
   while (!feof(competitorsFile)) {
     fprintf(printer, "%-12s", competitorRecord.name);
     fprintf(printer, "%4d", competitorRecord.age);
     fprintf(printer, "%3c", competitorRecord.gender);
     fprintf(printer, "\n");
     fread(&competitorRecord, sizeof(CompetitorStructure),
                                   1, competitorsFile);
   }
   fclose(competitorsFile);
   fclose(printer);
}
```

First, we give a name to the printer device. On many small computer systems this device is known as LPT1 (1 – the number not the letter); it may be different on your computer system.

```
#define printerDevice "LPT1"
```

The printer is regarded as a file. And so it is defined, opened and closed just like a file is.

```
FILE *printer = fopen(printerDevice, "w");

fclose(printer);
```

Notice that the open mode is *"w"*; this stands for write text mode.

*fprintf* converts and formats its arguments and outputs text just like *printf* does. But *fprintf* outputs its text onto the named file. In this example, the named file represents the printer.

```
fprintf(printer, "%-12s  ", competitorRecord.name);
```

*Exercise 8.2*

1 Write and test a program which will display the contents of the bicycle file created in exercise 8.1 on the printer.  Note: if your printer is attached to a network, you might (or you might not) need to press the three keys marked Ctrl, Alt and PrintScreen simultaneously to force the output to the printer; this should be done when your program run has finished.

2 When the police recover a bicycle, they might wish to contact the owner. Write and test a program which will input a bicycle frame number, search through the bicycle file created in program 8.1, and, if found in the file, outputs the owner's name and date of birth.  Your program should output a suitable message if a record for the recovered bicycle is not found in the file. A possible method is

```
input theFrameNumber
store FALSE in found
open the bicycleFile
retrieve the first bicycleRecord
while not at the end of the bicycleFile
 if theFrameNumber is the same as the bicycleRecord.frameNumber then
   store TRUE in found
   display the bicycleRecord
 endif
 retrieve the next bicycleRecord
endwhile
close the bicycleFile
if found still contains the value FALSE
   display "No registered owner found for this bicycle."
endif
```

### 8.7   Maintaining a File

The contents of files do not usually remain the same for long. For example, in a file of entries for the marathon, some entries will be withdrawn, some new ones included, some people may change their name or address or corrections to some records might be needed. Let us list some of the operations the organiser might wish to perform on the competitors' file

- remove a competitor's record
- include a new competitor's record
- print out all the competitor records in record number order
- print out the competitors records for a given category
- find a competitor's record from their competitor number
- change a competitor's record

The organiser's view of the program is a menu which provides the required operations.

We shall consider the programmer's view of the program shortly. But for now we shall consider just the user's view.

Let us design, write and test a general-purpose function which displays a menu and returns a valid choice selected by the user at the keyboard.

```
char choiceFromMenu(char menu[], char validChoices[]);
/* Displays menu on the screen.                         */
/* post-condition: returns a value from validChoices    */
/*                 selected by the user at the keyboard. */
```

An example of a call to this function is

```
char menu[] =   "               Menu\n\n"
                "    1   Add a new competitor\n"
                "    2   Remove a competitor\n"
                "    3   List all competitors\n"
                "    9   Quit\n\n"
                "    Your choice? ";
```

```
char validChoices[] = "1,2,3,9";
char choice = choiceFromMenu(menu, validChoices);
```

The C compiler joins together (that is, concatenates) adjacent string literals. So

```
                "               Menu\n\n"
                "    1   Add a new competitor\n"
                "    2   Remove a competitor\n"
                "    3   List all competitors\n"
                "    9   Quit\n\n"
                "    Your choice? ";
```

becomes one long string.

Now let us look at the function itself. Obtaining a choice from the keyboard is easy. The problem is determining whether the value input is also in the string of valid choices. The *strchr* function does just that. An example of a call to *strchr* is

```
returnedValue = strchr(string, character);
```

The *strchr* function from the *string* library searches for *character* (including the *NULL* character) within *string*. It returns *NULL* if *character* is not found in *string*, otherwise, it returns the address of the first occurrence of *character* in *string*. *strchr* is used in the *choiceFromMenu* function shown below.

```
char choiceFromMenu(char menu[], char validChoices[])
{
  enum { false };

  char choice[BUFSIZ];
  int choiceIsOK = false;

  while (!choiceIsOK) {
    printf("%s", menu);
    gets(choice);
    choiceIsOK = ((strlen(choice) != 0) &&
              (strchr(validChoices, choice[0]) != NULL));
  }
  printf("\n");
  return choice[0];
}
```

Now, why check for string length equal to zero? If the user just pressed return in response to the menu of options, then choice would contain just the end-of-string character – *NULL*. *validChoices* also contains the end-of-string character. We do not want this character to be regarded as a valid choice. So we ensure that if the length of the string is zero (remember that the *NULL* character is not counted) then the user's choice is not valid.

Based on the organiser's view we might draw the program structure chart like that shown in Figure 8.2.

Let us look at the problem from the programmer's point of view. We are basically dealing with competitor structure variables and the competitors file. What do we need to do?

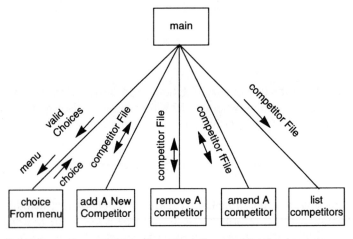

**Figure 8.2**  Possible program structure based on the organiser's view.

- fill a competitor structure variable with values from the keyboard
- write the contents of a competitor structure variable on the screen
- fill a competitor structure variable with values from the competitor file
- write the contents of a competitor structure variable onto the competitor file.

Let us design and write functions to do these tasks. We start with the function *competitorFromKeyboard*. Its specification is

```
CompetitorStructure competitorFromKeyboard(void);
/* Post-condition:  returns a competitor record entered */
/*                  at the keyboard.                    */
```

An example of a call to *competitorFromKeyboard* is

```
CompetitorStructure newCompetitor = competitorFromKeyboard();
```

Its implementation is very straightforward.

```
CompetitorStructure competitorFromKeyboard(void)
{
   CompetitorStructure competitor;

   readArrayOfChar("Competitor name? ", competitor.name);
   competitor.age = intNumberRead("Age? ");
   competitor.gender = charRead("Gender (m/f)? ");
   return competitor;
}
```

To write a competitor's record on the screen is also straightforward and is not described here.

Now we look at retrieving a competitor from the file. The organiser identifies each competitor by their competitor number; no two competitors have the same number. Fortunately for us as programmers, C automatically numbers each structure (or record) in a file, starting with zero.

```
record
Number     name          age gender

   0       Cartwright    29  f
   1       Jones         45  m
   2       Stevenson     51  m
   3       Patel         29  f
```

We make the convenient connection between competitor number and record number: they both represent the same thing. We use the record number to directly access a particular record without first retrieving and examining every preceding record. The *stdio* library function *fseek* does this for us.

*fseek* sets the file-position indicator: this is the point in the file where the next read or write is to take place. An example of a call to *fseek* is

```
fseek(competitorFile, recordNumber *
                    sizeof(CompetitorStructure), SEEK_SET);
```

The effect of *SEEK_SET* is to set the beginning of the file as the starting point for the file-position indicator. *SEEK_SET* is defined in the *stdio* library.

We use *fseek* in the implementation of *competitorFromFile*.

```
CompetitorStructure competitorFromFile(FILE *competitorFile,
                                            long recordNumber)
{
  CompetitorStructure competitor;

  fseek(competitorFile, recordNumber *
                    sizeof(CompetitorStructure),SEEK_SET);
  fread(&competitor, sizeof(CompetitorStructure), 1,
                                        competitorFile);
  return competitor;
}
```

There is one important restriction: it would be an error to seek past the end of the file. We have to decide upon, and fix, the maximum size of the file and hence the last record number **before** we use *fseek*. So, we modify *compet.h* accordingly and create a file of blank records (otherwise, how can the last record number exist?).

```
/* compet.h - contains competitor file record structure */
/*            and external file name.                    */


#include <stdio.h>


#define competitorDiskFileName "compet.dat"

typedef struct {
  char name[BUFSIZ];
  int age;
  char gender;
} CompetitorStructure;

#define lastRecordNumber 10L
```

Here, for our convenience, we have defined the last record number to be ten. In practice, of course, the last record number would be several hundred or even thousand.

```
/* program 8.4 - creates a file of blank competitor records. */


#include <stdio.h>
#include "compet.h"


void main(void)
{
   CompetitorStructure  competitor  =  {  "x",  0,  'x'  };
   FILE *competitorFile = fopen(competitorDiskFileName,"wb");
   long recordNumber = 0L;


   while (recordNumber <= lastRecordNumber) {
     fwrite(&competitor, sizeof(CompetitorStructure), 1,
                                           competitorFile);
     recordNumber++;
   }
   fclose(competitorFile);
}
```

Look at the line

```
CompetitorStructure competitor = {  "x", 0, 'x' };
```

Here, the *name* field is initialised with the string *x* (notice the double quotes) the *age* field with zero and the *gender* field with the character *x* (notice the single quotes).

Now we write the specification for *competitorFromFile*.

```
CompetitorStructure competitorFromFile(const FILE
                   *competitorFile, long recordNumber);
/* Pre-condition:   recordNumber is between 0 and        */
/*                  lastRecordNumber inclusive.          */
/* Post-condition:  returns the record at location       */
/*                  recordNumber in competitor file.     */
```

The converse of *competitorFromFile* is *writeCompetitorToFile*. The specification for *writeCompetitorToFile* is

```
void writeCompetitorToFile(FILE *competitorFile,
                           CompetitorStructure competitor,
                           long recordNumber);
/* Post-condition: competitorFile' record located at      */
/*                 recordNumber is replaced with           */
/*                 competitor.                             */
```

And here is its implementation

```
void writeCompetitorToFile(FILE *competitorFile,
                           CompetitorStructure competitor,
                           long recordNumber)
{
   fseek(competitorFile, recordNumber *
                  sizeof(CompetitorStructure), SEEK_SET);
   fwrite(&competitor, sizeof(CompetitorStructure), 1,
                                          competitorFile);
}
```

Now for the pay off. We shall amend a competitor's record by first retrieving it from the file and then replacing it with the updated record. The record to be replaced is identified by the record or competitor number.

```
/* Change a competitor's record. */
recordNumber = recordNumberFromKeyboard();
competitor = competitorFromFile(competitorFile,
                                          recordNumber);
writeCompetitorToScreen(competitor);
competitor = competitorFromKeyboard();
writeCompetitorToFile(competitorFile, competitor,
                                          recordNumber);
```

The implementation of other organiser-defined requirements are just as easy. To remove a competitor's record, we overwrite it with the null record, as used in the file creation program.

```
/* Remove a competitor. */
CompetitorStructure nullRecord = { "x", 0, 'x' };
recordNumber = recordNumberFromKeyboard();
writeCompetitorToFile(competitorFile, nullRecord,
                                          recordNumber);
```

We include a new competitor in the file by finding the first record number whose name field contains the string *"x"* and then overwrite the record in the file with the new competitor details.

```
/* Add a new competitor. */
recordNumber = nextFreeRecordNumber(competitorFile);
if (recordNumber < 0L)
  printf("No room in file for another competitor\n");
else {
  newCompetitor = competitorFromKeyboard();
  writeCompetitorToFile(competitorFile, newCompetitor,
                                        recordNumber);
}
```

To list all competitors, we retrieve the data stored for each record number in turn.

```
/* List all competitors. */
recordNumber = 0L;
while (recordNumber <= lastRecordNumber) {
  competitor = competitorFromFile(competitorFile,
                                        recordNumber);
  printf("%3ld  ", recordNumber);
  writeCompetitorToScreen(competitor);
  recordNumber++;
}
```

However, to find a competitor's number when given just their name, we have to search through the entire file from beginning to end, record-by-record. Every time we find a matching name we print the record together with its corresponding record number. We set the file-position indicator to the beginning of the file with rewind

```
rewind(competitorFile);
```

And then process the entire file using the ordinary sequential method described in section 8.2.

```
/* Find a competitor's number. */
recordNumber = 0L;
readArrayOfChar("Competitor's name? ", aName);
rewind(competitorFile);
fread(&competitor, sizeof(CompetitorStructure), 1,
                                        competitorFile);
while (!feof(competitorFile)) {
  if (strcmp(competitor.name, aName) == 0) {
    printf("%3ld  ", recordNumber);
    writeCompetitorToScreen(competitor);
  }
```

```
        recordNumber++;
        fread(&competitor, sizeof(CompetitorStructure), 1,
                                            competitorFile);
   }
```

Here is the entire program.

```
    /* program 8.5 - maintains competitor file. */

    #include <stdio.h>
    #include <string.h>
    #include <stdlib.h>
    #include <ctype.h>
    #include "compet.h"


char charRead(char prompt[]);
/* Post-condition: returns a char entered at the keyboard. */


char choiceFromMenu(char menu[], char validChoices[]);
/* Displays menu, returns a valid choice. */


CompetitorStructure competitorFromFile(FILE
                    *competitorFile, long recordNumber);
/* Pre-condition:   recordNumber is between 0 and      */
/*                  lastRecordNumber inclusive.        */
/* Post-condition:  returns the record at location     */
/*                  recordNumber in competitor file.   */


CompetitorStructure competitorFromKeyboard(void);
/* Post-condition: returns a competitor record entered */
/*                 at the keyboard.                    */


void getCategory(int *min, int *max);
/* *min' and *max' contain values input by the user at */
/* the keyboard.                                       */


int  intNumberRead(char prompt[]);
/* Post-condition: returns number entered at the       */
/* keyboard.                                           */
```

```
long longNumberRead(char prompt[]);
/* Post-condition: returns number entered at the       */
/* keyboard.                                            */


long nextFreeRecordNumber(FILE *competitorFile);
/* Post-condition: returns the next free competitor     */
/*                 number in competitorFile - if there  */
/*                 is one, otherwise returns -1.         */


void readArrayOfChar(char prompt[], char array[]);
/* Post-condition: array' contains characters entered    */
/* at the keyboard.                                      */


long recordNumberFromKeyboard(void);
/* Post-condition: returns a number between 0 and        */
/*                 lastRecordNumber inclusive input by   */
/*                 the user at the keyboard.             */

void writeCompetitorToFile(FILE *competitorFile,
                           CompetitorStructure competitor,
                           long recordNumber);
/* Post-condition: competitorFile' record located at     */
/*                 recordNumber is replaced with         */
/*                 competitor.                           */



void writeCompetitorToScreen(
                        CompetitorStructure competitor);
/* Displays competitor on screen. */

void main(void)
{
  enum { false, true };

  char aName[BUFSIZ];
  int minAge, maxAge;
  long recordNumber;

  FILE *competitorFile = fopen(competitorDiskFileName, "r+b");
  CompetitorStructure competitor;
  CompetitorStructure nullRecord = { "x", 0, 'x' };
```

```
char menu[] = "\n\n"
"          Menu\n\n"
"    1   Add a new competitor\n"
"    2   Remove a competitor\n"
"    3   List all competitors in competitor number order\n"
"    4   List all competitors in a category\n"
"    5   Find a competitor's number\n"
"    6   Change a competitor's details\n"
"    9   Quit\n\n"
"    Your choice? ";


char validChoices[] = "1,2,3,4,5,6,9";
char choice = choiceFromMenu(menu, validChoices);


int isDone = (choice == '9');


if (competitorFile == NULL) {
  printf("Program halted: unable to open %s\n",
         competitorDiskFileName);
  exit(EXIT_FAILURE);
}
while (!isDone) {
  switch (choice) {


  case '1':  /* Add a new competitor. */
    recordNumber = nextFreeRecordNumber(competitorFile);
    if (recordNumber < 0L)
      printf("No room in file for another competitor\n");
    else {
      competitor = competitorFromKeyboard();
      writeCompetitorToFile(competitorFile, competitor,
                                            recordNumber);
    }
    break;


  case '2':  /* Remove a competitor. */
    recordNumber = recordNumberFromKeyboard();
    writeCompetitorToFile(competitorFile, nullRecord,
                                          recordNumber);
    break;
```

```
case '3':  /* List all competitors. */
   recordNumber = 0L;
   while (recordNumber <= lastRecordNumber) {
      competitor = competitorFromFile(competitorFile,
                                         recordNumber);
      printf("%31d  ", recordNumber);
      writeCompetitorToScreen(competitor);
      recordNumber++;
   }
   break;



case '4':  /* List all competitors in a category. */
   getCategory(&minAge, &maxAge);
   recordNumber = 0L;
   while (recordNumber <= lastRecordNumber) {
      competitor = competitorFromFile(competitorFile,
                                         recordNumber);
      if  ((competitor.age >= minAge) &&
                     (competitor.age <= maxAge)) {
         printf("%31d  ", recordNumber);
         writeCompetitorToScreen(competitor);
      }
      recordNumber++;
   }
   break;



case '5':  /* Find a competitor's number. */
   recordNumber = 0L;
   readArrayOfChar("Competitor's name? ", aName);
   rewind(competitorFile);
   fread(&competitor, sizeof(CompetitorStructure), 1,
                     competitorFile);
   while (!feof(competitorFile)) {
      if (strcmp(competitor.name, aName) == 0) {
         printf("%31d  ", recordNumber);
         writeCompetitorToScreen(competitor);
      }
      recordNumber++;
      fread(&competitor, sizeof(CompetitorStructure),
                                 1, competitorFile);
   }
   break;
```

```
      case '6':   /* change a competitor's details. */
        recordNumber = recordNumberFromKeyboard();
        competitor = competitorFromFile(competitorFile,
                                        recordNumber);
        writeCompetitorToScreen(competitor);
        competitor = competitorFromKeyboard();
        writeCompetitorToFile(competitorFile, competitor,
                              recordNumber);
      break;

      case '9':   /* Quit. */
        isDone = true;
        break;

      default:
        printf("main: This should not happen!\n");
        break;
      }
      choice = choiceFromMenu(menu, validChoices);
      isDone = (choice == '9');
    }

}

char charRead(char prompt[])
{
  char string[BUFSIZ];

  printf("%s", prompt);
  gets(string);
  return string[0];
}

char choiceFromMenu(char menu[], char validChoices[])
{
  enum { false };
  char choice[BUFSIZ];
  int choiceIsOK = false;

  while (!choiceIsOK) {
    printf("%s", menu);
    gets(choice);
    choiceIsOK = ((strlen(choice) != 0) &&
                  (strchr(validChoices, choice[0]) != NULL));
  }
```

```c
   printf("\n");
   return choice[0];
}


CompetitorStructure competitorFromFile(FILE
                  *competitorFile, long recordNumber)
{
   CompetitorStructure competitor;

   fseek(competitorFile, recordNumber *
                  sizeof(CompetitorStructure), SEEK_SET);
   fread(&competitor, sizeof(CompetitorStructure), 1,
                                      competitorFile);
   return competitor;
}



CompetitorStructure competitorFromKeyboard(void)
{
   CompetitorStructure competitor;

   readArrayOfChar("Competitor name? ", competitor.name);
   competitor.age = intNumberRead("Age? ");
   competitor.gender = charRead("Gender (m/f)? ");
   return competitor;
}


void getCategory(int *min, int *max)
{
   char category;

   category = tolower(charRead(
        "Category - junior, regular or senior (j/r/s)? "));
   if (category == 'j')
     *min = 10, *max = 15;
   else if (category == 'r')
     *min = 16, *max = 39;
   else *min = 40, *max = 99;
   printf("\n");
}
```

```
int  intNumberRead(char prompt[])
{
   char string[BUFSIZ];
   int number = 0;


   printf("%s", prompt);
   gets(string);
   sscanf(string, "%d", &number);
   return number;
}



long longNumberRead(char prompt[])
{
   char string[BUFSIZ];
   long number = 0L;

   printf("%s", prompt);
   gets(string);
   sscanf(string, "%ld", &number);
   return number;
}



long nextFreeRecordNumber(FILE *competitorFile)
{
   CompetitorStructure competitor;
   long recordNumber = 0L;


   rewind(competitorFile);
   fread(&competitor, sizeof(CompetitorStructure), 1,
                                          competitorFile);
   while (!feof(competitorFile)) {
      if (strcmp(competitor.name, "x") == 0)
         return recordNumber;
      recordNumber++;
      fread(&competitor, sizeof(CompetitorStructure), 1,
                                          competitorFile);
   }
   return -1;  /* no free record numbers left in the file. */
}
```

```c
void readArrayOfChar(char prompt[], char array[])
{
  printf("%s", prompt);
  gets(array);
}



long recordNumberFromKeyboard()
{
  long n = longNumberRead("Competitor number? ");
  while ((n < 0) && (n > lastRecordNumber)) {
    printf(
          "Competitor number must be between 0 and %ld\n",
                                      lastRecordNumber);
    n = longNumberRead("Competitor number? ");
  }
  return n;
}



void writeCompetitorToFile(FILE *competitorFile,
                      CompetitorStructure competitor,
                      long recordNumber)
{
  fseek(competitorFile, recordNumber *
                  sizeof(CompetitorStructure), SEEK_SET);
  fwrite(&competitor, sizeof(CompetitorStructure), 1,
                                      competitorFile);
}



void writeCompetitorToScreen(
                      CompetitorStructure competitor)
{
  printf("%s,  %d,  %c\n", competitor.name,
                          competitor.age,
                          competitor.gender);
}
/****** End Of Program 8.4 ******/
```

In *main*, the file is opened with

```c
FILE *competitorFile = fopen(competitorDiskFileName, "r+b");
```

*"r+b"* specifies that a file, which already exists, is to be updated. So, before running program 8.5, we must first create the *competitorFile* by running program 8.4.

In the *getCategory* function, we have used the comma operator to help make the layout clearer. (Without the comma operator, braces would be needed to group each pair of assignment statements.)

```
if (category == 'j')
   *min = 10, *max = 15;
else if (category == 'r')
   *min = 16, *max = 39;
else *min = 40, *max = 99;
```

The success of the *nextFreeRecordNumber* function depends on the *name* field containing just *"x"*. So this function is tightly coupled to the file creation program and to the processes (in *main*) which remove a competitor's record from the file.

The validation in the *recordNumberFromKeyboard* function is essential because it is up to us to ensure that a record actually exists for the record number specified.

## 8.8  Documentation

File content and record structure are described in data dictionaries – see Figure 8.1 for an example.

Formatted printed output is described on printer format sheets. An example is shown in Figure 8.3. Field widths, in which data values are to be printed, are shown as two crosses joined by a straight line.

## 8.9  Programming Principles

Perhaps the best way of managing files is to

- fix their maximum size at the beginning
- create the file with dummy records
- put data onto the file by overwriting a dummy record
- remove data from the file by overwriting the record with dummy data
- access the records either sequentially or directly as required.

Remember that direct access methods can be used only on files which already exist.

When you need to perform the same operation on each and every record in a file, you will need to use a sequential access method: start with the first record in the file, retrieve and process it and then go on to the next record. Repeat the process for each record in turn.

When you need to perform an operation on a particular record in the file, you will need to use a direct access method: use *fseek* to set the file position indicator to the required record number. Remember that both *fread* and *fwrite* automatically advance the file position indicator after they have retrieved or written a record.

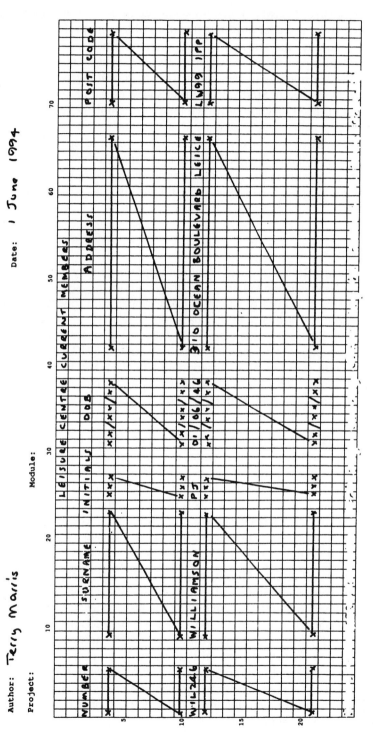

**Figure 8.3**

When trying to decide what functions are needed, concentrate on the data involved. For each data type, consider providing functions which input values from the keyboard and output them on the screen. Provide functions which deal only with records or structures. And supply functions which control file input and output.

Develop your programs incrementally, that is, repeatedly add a little bit to your program and then test it. Start with the user's view of the program, for example, the menu. Then for each function provide a temporary implementation - just a message announcing the name of the function and inviting the user to press a key to return to the menu. In this way you can test the menu before proceeding any further. Then take a function – any will do – complete and test it. Repeat for each function. This means that you are never very far away from a program which compiles and runs. It may not do all that it is supposed to do. But at least it will run and you will know which parts of it require completion.

*Exercise 8.3*

1 The Skip Hire Company (SHC) rent out skips for hire by trade and public alike. When a person wishes to hire a skip, they contact the SHC office and give their name, address, nature of waste to be disposed (e.g. garden waste, builder's rubble) and the size of the skip required (e.g. mini, standard or maxi). SHC allocate a skip to the customer and deliver it to them on the required day. When the customer has filled the skip, they contact SHC who then collect it and dispose of its contents at an appropriate site. The skip is then allocated to the pool of available skips. If a skip becomes irreparably damaged then it is scrapped and replaced with a new skip. Every skip is replaced after being used for three years.

   (a) Design a record structure for storing data on any one skip.
   (b) Design and implement a menu that will enable the skip hire manager to manage the allocation, delivery, collection and replacement of skips. The manager should also be able to print out the location of each skip.
   (c) Create a file of about 20 blank or dummy skip records designed in (a).
   (d) Complete a program which will maintain a file of skip records. The program should include functions which will add a new skip to the file, remove an old skip from the file and amend the contents of a skip record.

2 Create a file of about 100 employee records. Each employee record should contain name, department and annual salary details. Then design and write a program which will print the contents of the file on the printer. The printer output should be paged. There should be a heading on each page, as well as a page number and column headings. At the bottom of each page there should be a summary total of the salaries on that page. In addition, the last page should include the total number of employees and the total annual salary bill. Of course, the headings should not creep up (or down) successive pages. You will need to decide on the maximum number of records to be printed on a page. One way of proceeding might be

```
retrieve first record from file
while not at end of file
  if (at top of page) or (past last record position on page) then
    new page functions
  endif
  print a record
  if (past last record position on page) then
    bottom of page functions
  endif
  retrieve next record from file
endwhile
```

# 9

# Text Files

## 9.1 Introduction

In Chapters 7 and 8 we looked at files with fixed-length records. Now we look at files with variable-length records. The problem with variable-length records is knowing where one record ends and the next one begins. One method is to use a special character to mark the end of a record. We see how this might be done with a file of text.

A file of text is a sequence of characters structured into lines. A line is terminated with either a newline character or the end of file character. For example

Now sleeps the crimson petal\nNow the white ^z

$\uparrow$ newline character    $\uparrow$ end-of-file character

(The end-of-file character is usually ^z in MS-DOS systems and ^d on Unix systems.)

Program 9.1 shown below retrieves lines of text from a file (such as a C program) and writes them out on the printer.

```
/* program 9.1 - prints text files. */
#include <stdio.h>
#include <stdlib.h>

#define printerDevice "LPT1"

void main(void)
{
   char diskFileName[BUFSIZ], line[BUFSIZ];
   FILE *text;
   FILE *printer = fopen(printerDevice, "w");
```

```
printf("Name of file to print? ");
gets(diskFileName);
text = fopen(diskFileName, "r");
if (text == NULL) {
  printf("Program halted: unable to ");
  printf("find %s to print.\n", diskFileName);
  exit(EXIT_FAILURE);
}
while (fgets(line, BUFSIZ, text) != NULL)
  fprintf(printer, "%s", line);
fclose(text);
fclose(printer);
}
```

The line

```
fgets(line, BUFSIZ, text);
```

says retrieve characters from the file named *text* and place them in the variable *line* until either *BUFSIZ - 1* characters have been read or the newline character has been retrieved or the end of the file *text* has been reached; then append *NULL* to the character sequence stored in line. The newline and end-of-file characters retrieved from the file are discarded. *fgets* returns *NULL* if the end of the file is reached. So

```
while (fgets(line, BUFSIZ, text) != NULL)
```

makes repeated calls to *fgets* until the end of the file is reached. *fgets* works just like *gets* does, except that *gets* obtains text from the keyboard while *fgets* obtains text from a named file.

*fprintf* works just like *printf* does, except that the output is to the named file (*text*, in this example) and not the screen.

## 9.2 Command Line Arguments

When program 9.1 is run, it requests the user to input the name of the file to be printed. What we would like to do is supply the name of the file to be printed at the time we run the file print program. For example, suppose the file print program was named *pprint* (for pretty print) and the file to be printed was named *prog91.c*, then we would like to issue the command

```
pprint prog91.c
```

at the operating system prompt. We would like the string *prog91.c* to be input into the *pprint* program. The following program shows how this may be done.

```
/* pprint - prints text files, uses command line arguments. */

#include <stdio.h>
#include <stdlib.h>

#define printerDevice "LPT1"


void printTextFile(char diskFileName[]);
/* Writes contents of diskFileName in printer. */


void main(int argumentCount, char *pArgumentValues[])
{
  if (argumentCount != 2) {
    printf("Usage: pprint filename.ext\n");
    exit(EXIT_FAILURE);
  }
  printTextFile(pArgumentValues[1]);
}


void printTextFile(char diskFileName[])
{
  char line[BUFSIZ];
  FILE *printer = fopen(printerDevice, "w");
  FILE *text = fopen(diskFileName, "r");

  if (text == NULL) {
    printf("Program halted: unable to find %s\n",
                            diskFileName);
    exit(EXIT_FAILURE);
  }
  while (fgets(line, BUFSIZ, text) != NULL)
    fprintf(printer, "%s", line);
  fclose(text);
  fclose(printer);
}
```

The essential point is the way *main* is written. Here, *main* has two parameters, *argumentCount* and *\*pArgumentValues[]*.

*pArgumentValues* points to an array of pointers to strings. For example, if at the operating system prompt we entered *pprint prog91.c*, then *pArgumentValues* contains the address of an array of pointers, where each pointer contains the address of a string entered.

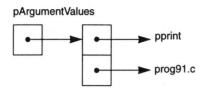

*pArgumentValues[0]* points to *pprint*. *pArgumentValues[1]* points to *prog91.c*. These strings can be used within a program and are known as program parameters.

*argumentCount* contains the number of strings in the array to which *pArgumentValues* points. If the user uses *pprint* incorrectly, by not supplying it with the name of a file to be printed for example, then *argumentCount* does not contain the value *2* and the user is informed how to use *pprint* correctly.

### Exercise 9.1

**1** Write a program which will print out program text files. There should be a margin of about 1 inch (25 mm) all round the printed text on each page. If a line of text is too long to fit across the page, then the line should be truncated and two exclamation marks should be printed. Each page should have its own title and page number. You could use program *pprint* as a starting point. Note: if you use an integrated programming environment, then you might need to exit from the environment to run the program.

### 9.3  File Handling Program Structure

Every file is managed by the same few processes: open, close, retrieve, write and error handling. If we confine, to a single function, all the logic necessary to open a file, retrieve data from it and then close it, then we can use the same function with minimal modification to retrieve data from any other file. Let us see how this might be done.

We can think of the file as being in one of three states: either unopened (that is, never been opened in the current program run) or open (ready for retrieving records) or closed (because the end of the file has been reached).

If the file is unopened, then we want to open it and set its state to open.

If the file is open, then we want to retrieve a record. If the retrieval fails, because the end of the file has been reached for example, then we want to close the file and set its state to closed.

A file, once closed, cannot be opened again in the current program run. Here is how we might write the function.

```
void retrieveLineFromTextFile(char diskFileName[],
                        char lineOfText[], int *pFinished)
{
   enum { false, true };
   typedef enum { unopened, open, closed } FileState;
```

```
static FILE *file;
static FileState fileState = unopened;

*pFinished = false;
switch (fileState) {
case unopened:
  file = fopen(diskFileName, "r");
  if (file == NULL) {
    printf("Unable to open %s\n", diskFileName);
    exit(EXIT_FAILURE);
  }
  else
    fileState = open;   /* fall through */
case open:
  if (fgets(lineOfText, BUFSIZ, file) == NULL) {
    fclose(file);
    *pFinished = true;
    fileState = closed;
  }
  break;
case closed:
  break;
default:
  printf(
"retrieveLineFromTextFile: this should not happen.\n");
  exit(EXIT_FAILURE);
}

}
```

When the function is called for the first time, the file state is *unopened*. An attempt is made to open the file. If successful then the file state is *open* and we fall through to the next case.

We attempt to retrieve a record with *fgets*. Let us suppose we are successful. We return to the caller.

On the next call to the function, the value stored in *fileState* is still open. This is the result of declaring the type *FileState* as *static*. Variables whose storage class is defined as *static* remain in existence from one function call to the next. Without the static storage class specifier, the variable *fileState* would be re-created and re-initialised with *unopened* every time the function was called.

So the file state is *open* and we attempt to retrieve a record. If we fail, because the end of the file has been reached for example, then we close the file, set *\*pFinished* to true and the file state to *closed*. We need to communicate to other functions the fact that the end of the file has been reached; this is the purpose of the *int \*pFinished* parameter.

If we make a further call to *retrieveLineFromTextFile*, the file state is *closed* and no further action is specified.

The function to manage the printer works in a similar way. It is shown in program 9.3.

```
/* program 9.3 - prints text files, uses functions. */



#include <stdio.h>
#include <stdlib.h>



void retrieveLineFromTextFile(char diskFileName[],
                    char lineOfText[], int *pFinished);
/* Post-condition: *pFinished' = true if the end of the */
/*                file diskFilename is reached,          */
/*                otherwise lineOfText' contains a       */
/*                line of text.                          */



void writeLineToPrinter(char lineOfText[], int finished);
/* Writes lineOfText to the printer if finished is       */
/* not true.                                             */



void main(void)
{
   char line[BUFSIZ], diskFileName[BUFSIZ];
   int finished;



   printf("Name of text file to print? ");
   gets(diskFileName);
   retrieveLineFromTextFile(diskFileName, line, &finished);
   while (!finished) {
     writeLineToPrinter(line, finished);
     retrieveLineFromTextFile(diskFileName, line, &finished);
   }
}
```

```
void retrieveLineFromTextFile(char diskFileName[],
                        char lineOfText[], int *pFinished)
{
   enum { false, true };
   typedef enum { unopened, open, closed } FileState;

   static FILE *file;
   static FileState fileState = unopened;

   *pFinished = false;


   switch (fileState) {

   case unopened:
     file = fopen(diskFileName, "r");
     if (file == NULL) {
       printf("Unable to open %s\n", diskFileName);
       exit(EXIT_FAILURE);
     }
     else
       fileState = open;   /* fall through */
   case open:
     if (fgets(lineOfText, BUFSIZ, file) == NULL) {
       fclose(file);
       *pFinished = true;
       fileState = closed;
     }
     break;
   case closed:
     break;
   default:
     printf(
   "retrieveLineFromTextFile: this should not happen.\n");
     exit(EXIT_FAILURE);
   }
}


void writeLineToPrinter(char lineOfText[], int finished)
{
   typedef enum { unopened, open, closed } FileState;

   static FILE *printer;
   static FileState fileState = unopened;
```

```
      switch (fileState) {
      case unopened:
        printer = fopen("LPT1", "w");
        if (printer == NULL) {
          printf("Unable to open printer.\n");
          exit(EXIT_FAILURE);
        }
        else
          fileState = open;   /* fall through */
      case open:
        if (!finished)
          fprintf(printer, "%s", lineOfText);
        else {
          fclose(printer);
          fileState = closed;
        }
        break;


      case closed:
        break;
      default:
        printf(
              "writeLineToPrinter: this should not happen.\n");
        exit(EXIT_FAILURE);
        break;
      }
  }
```

*writeLineToPrinter* needs to know when to close the printer file. This is why *finished* is a parameter to the function. Notice the role of *finished* in *main*.

Notice also that *main* has nothing to do with opening files and then closing them. This is all taken care of in the retrieve and write functions. Very neat.

## 9.4  Processing Text Files

It is sometimes convenient to create files using an ordinary text editor (such as the one you use to create or amend your programs). For example, suppose the following data on people who owe money were stored in a text file

```
147309 Cartwright £19999.99
247609 Jones £20000.00
965235 Stevenson £20000.01
```

Each line in the file has the format *referenceNumber name debt*. We can write programs which use these data. Suppose we want to create a file of debtors who owe more than, say, £19999.99. We need to isolate the *debt* from a line of text in order to decide whether the line should go in the new file. For example, we need to isolate *19999.99* from

```
147309 Cartwright £19999.99
```

We could write our own function from scratch to do the job. Or we could use the *strtok* function from the *string* library.

strtok divides a string into a set of words known as tokens. Its template is

```
char *strtok(char *string, const string *separators);
```

An example of a call to *strtok* is

```
char line[] = "147309 Cartwright £19999.99";
char wordSeparators[] = " ,£";
char *word;

word = strtok(line, wordSeparators);
```

*wordSeparators* is a string which contains the symbols which separate one word from the next. Here the explicit word separator characters are space, comma and the £ sign; the implicit word separator is the *NULL* end-of-string character.

word is a pointer to *char*; that is, it contains the start address of a sequence of characters held in memory.

strtok looks through *line* for a character which is not in *wordSeparators*. If it finds one then it is the first character in the first word in *line*. Then *strtok* looks through line for a character which is in *wordSeparators*. If it finds one then it is replaced with the *NULL* character to mark the end of the first word. *strtok* stores a pointer to the rest of the line and returns the address of the first word.

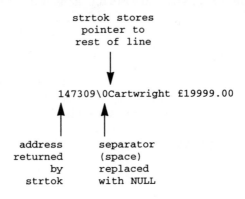

If we subsequently make the call

```
word = strtok(NULL, wordSeparators);
```

*strtok* looks through the rest of the line for a character which is in *wordSeparators*. If it finds one then it is replaced with the *NULL* character to mark the end of the next word. *strtok* stores a pointer to the rest of the line and returns the address of the next word.

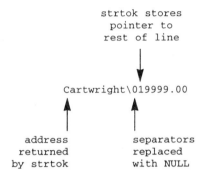

If, on looking through *line strtok* cannot find a character which is in *wordSeparators*, then it returns *NULL*.

Since *strtok* modifies its first string argument value, we are obliged to provide a copy of *line* for *strtok* to work with. This is what we have done in the function *debtFromLine* shown below.

```
char* debtFromLine(char aLine[])
{
   int wordCount = 0;
   char wordSeparators[] = " ,£";
   char *words[BUFSIZ] = { NULL };
   char *line = (char*)malloc(strlen(aLine) + 1);
   char *word;

   strcpy(line, aLine);
   word = strtok(line, wordSeparators);
   while (word != NULL) {
     wordCount++;
     words[wordCount] = word;
     word = strtok(NULL, wordSeparators);
   }
   return words[3];
}
```

What we have done here is to store pointers to each word in line.

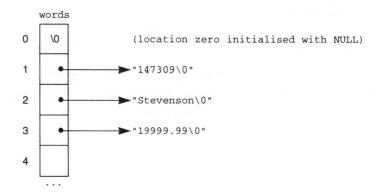

Program 9.4 creates a file of debtors who owe more than £19999.99 from the original file of debtors.

```
/* program 9.4 - processes debtors file to create a new */
/* file of debtors who owe more than £19999.99           */

#include <stdio.h>
#include <stdlib.h>
#include <string.h>


char* debtFromLine(char line[]);
/* Post-condition: returns debt from a line of text in */
/*                 debtor.dat.                          */

double doubleFromString(char string[]);
/* returns double number equivalent of string. */

void retrieveLineFromTextFile(char diskFileName[],
                char lineOfText[], int *pFinished);
/* Post-condition: *pFinished' = true if the end of the */
/*                 file diskFilename is reached,          */
/*                 otherwise lineOfText' contains a       */
/*                 line of text.                          */

void writeLineToTextFile(char diskFileName[],
                char lineOfText[], int finished);
/* Post-condition: lineOfText is written to file */
/*                 diskFileName if  finished = 0,  */
/*                 otherwise if finished = 1,       */
/*                 closes diskFileName.             */
```

```
void main(void)
{
  char line[BUFSIZ];
  int finished;
  char* debt;
  char debtorsDiskFileName[] = "debtors.dat";
  char bigDebtorsDiskFileName[] = "bigdebts.dat";

  retrieveLineFromTextFile(debtorsDiskFileName, line, &finished);
  while (!finished) {
    debt = debtFromLine(line);
    if (doubleFromString(debt) >= 20000.00)
      writeLineToTextFile(bigDebtorsDiskFileName, line,
                          finished);
    retrieveLineFromTextFile(debtorsDiskFileName, line,
                             &finished);
  }
}

char* debtFromLine(char aLine[])
{
  int wordCount = 0;
  char wordSeparators[] = " ,£";
  char *words[BUFSIZ] = { NULL };
  char *line = (char*)malloc(strlen(aLine) + 1);
  char *word;

  strcpy(line, aLine);

  word = strtok(line, wordSeparators);
  while (word != NULL) {
    wordCount++;
    words[wordCount] = word;
    word = strtok(NULL, wordSeparators);
  }
  return words[3];
}

double doubleFromString(char string[])
{
  double number = 0.0;

  sscanf(string, "%lf", &number);
  return number;
}
```

```c
void retrieveLineFromTextFile(char diskFileName[],
                      char lineOfText[], int *pFinished)
{
  enum { false, true };
  typedef enum { unopened, open, closed } FileState;

  static FILE *file;
  static FileState fileState = unopened;

  *pFinished = false;
  switch (fileState) {
  case unopened:
    file = fopen(diskFileName, "r");
    if (file == NULL) {
      printf("Unable to open %s\n", diskFileName);
      exit(EXIT_FAILURE);
    }
    else
      fileState = open;   /* fall through */
  case open:
    if (fgets(lineOfText, BUFSIZ, file) == NULL) {
      fclose(file);
      *pFinished = true;
      fileState = closed;
    }
    break;
  case closed:
    break;
  default:
    printf(
    "retrieveLineFromTextFile: this should not happen.\n");
    exit(EXIT_FAILURE);
  }
}



void writeLineToTextFile(char diskFileName[],
                      char lineOfText[], int finished)
{
  enum { false, true };
  typedef enum { unopened, open, closed } FileState;

  static FILE *file;
  static FileState fileState = unopened;
```

```
  switch (fileState) {
  case unopened:
    file = fopen(diskFileName, "w");
    if (file == NULL) {
      printf("Unable to open %s\n", diskFileName);
      exit(EXIT_FAILURE);
    }
    else
      fileState = open;    /* fall through */
  case open:
    if (!finished)
      fprintf(file, "%s", lineOfText);
    else {
      fclose(file);
      fileState = closed;
    }
    break;
  case closed:
    break;
  default:
    printf("retrieveLineFromTextFile: this should not
                                      happen.\n");
    exit(EXIT_FAILURE);
  }
}
```

After running this program the file *bigdebts.dat* contains

```
247609 Jones     £20000.00
965235 Stevenson £20000.01
```

## 9.5  Programming Principles

Place all the operations – open, close, input, output – which deal with one file – into one function. If a file handling error occurs, then the problem lies in one function.

When designing and writing programs, focus on the data values involved. Consider providing functions which operate on these values, operations such as input, output and creation. Then use these functions to create other (higher level) functions or programs.

If you need to write a function, see if somebody has already done it – if they have then use it. If you find a function which nearly does what you want, then adapt it. There is no need to re-invent what has already been invented.

*Exercise 9.2*

**1** Word processors usually embed formatting commands in the text. Unfortunately, different word processors have different formatting commands; this means that files created with one word processor may not be amended with another word processor. Write a program which will copy any file created by a word processor into a text file without the formatting commands. (The text file may then be formatted by any other word processor.)

# 10

# Screens

## 10.1 The User

The screen is an important means of communication between a program and its user. If the user does not like what he or she sees on the screen, then we should not be surprised if the user does not like the program. Even if the program is technically superb and functions perfectly, it would make no difference to the way the user views the program.

How the program works, from the user's point of view, is also important. If the program does not appear to work in the way the user wants it to work, then again, we should not be surprised if the user does not like it.

Programmers, people who write programs for other people to use, should understand what the user wants, even if the user does not know or cannot express it. Users usually know what they do not want when they see it.

## 10.2 The Screen Display

Let us start with some guiding principles.

Screen displays should

- use the same words as the user does
- reflect the user's way of working
- not annoy serious users
- be consistent
- contain no unnecessary features or clutter.

Screen displays should use the same words as the user does. For example, if a business uses the word "client" in a description of a business transaction, then we should not use another word such as "customer" to mean the same thing.

Screen displays should mirror the user's way of working. For example, if a user enters data taken from a handwritten form into a computer system, then the screen should look like the form; the data entry fields should be in the same relative position on both form and screen.

Screen displays should be appropriate to the intended user. Bright flashing colours, sound effects and slang may be suitable for a games program but would be out of place in an accounts package. Even boxes containing items such as menus, data entry forms and reports are found to be insulting by some users, perhaps because they find them patronising.

If your program uses several menus, then they should all look alike; they should all be in the same format, they should all appear in the same place on the screen and they should all use the same selection method. If one menu uses the word "Quit" to mean exit from the current menu, then all other menus should use the same word (Quit) for the same purpose. Help and instructions should always appear in the same place no matter how many different screens there are.

As a general rule, screens should contain the minimum to do the required job – nothing more; no frills, no fancy effects, just enough for the task.

## 10.3   Common Screen Formats

The typical personal computer (PC) screen can be considered as a rectangular grid comprising, say, 80 columns and 25 rows. A single character occupies one column width. One line of text occupies one row.

Figure 10.1 shows a simple menu. The points worthy of note are

- the menu is in the centre of the screen
- the menu is well spaced out and uses the available space
- descriptive headings are shown in upper case
- the options are shown in lower case
- the options are clearly separated from the headings by two blank lines
- the option numbers are separated from their captions by two spaces
- the line which invites the user to take some action stands out
- the inked-in block shows where the cursor is positioned ready for input
- the words used in the menu can be understood by any employee.

Perhaps it would be an improvement if the date and time were to be shown in, say, the top right corner.

Each of us has filled in a form of some kind. A form to be filled in on the screen looks just like a form to be filled in on paper. Look at Figure 10.2 overleaf and notice that

- the screen display has a title
- the data entry fields are shown by a ×————×
- the captions, headings or prompts end with a colon
- there are two spaces between caption and data entry field
- most captions are shown right justified with fields left justified
- some captions are shown left justified with fields right justified
- there are at least four spaces between a field and a following caption.

When the form first appears on the screen, the cursor is positioned at the beginning of the first data entry field. When the data have been entered and return pressed, the cursor skips to the next field.

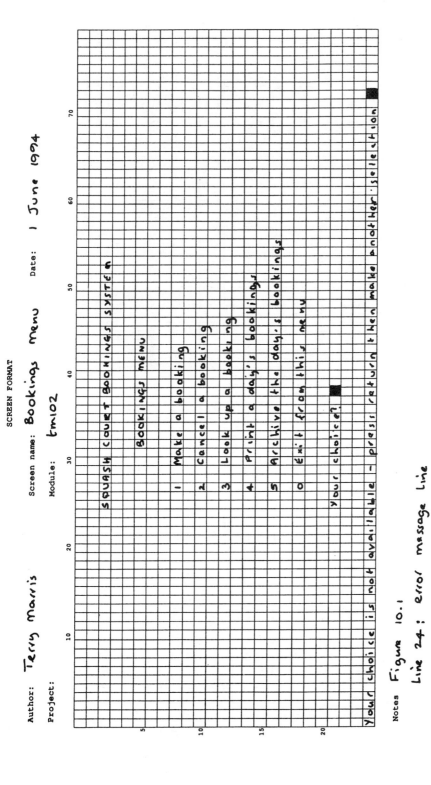

SCREEN FORMAT

Author: Terry Morris

Project:

Screen name: Bookings Menu    Date: 1 June 1994

Module: tm102

```
     SQUASH COURT BOOKINGS SYSTEM

     BOOKINGS MENU

 1   Make a booking

 2   Cancel a booking

 3   Look up a booking

 4   Print a day's bookings

 5   Archive the day's bookings

 0   Exit from this menu

     Your choice?

Your choice is not available - press return then make another selection
```

Notes Figure 10.1

Line 24 : error message line

**Figure 10.1**

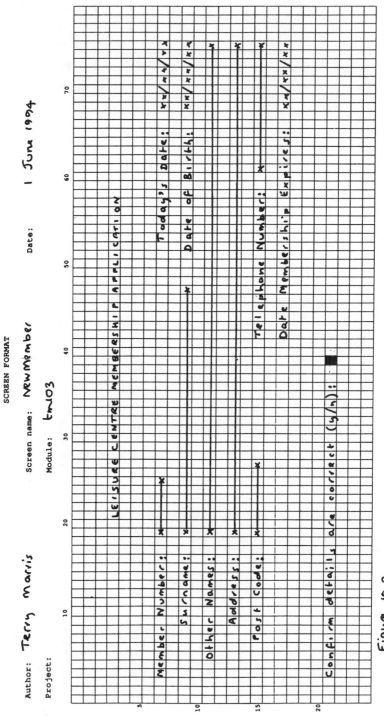

Figure 10.2

Sometimes, we need to show the contents of a file in table format. Look at Figure 10.3 on the next page for example. Note the following points

- the column headings are written in upper case
- the column headings are centrally placed over their data entries
- the data entries are centrally placed under their column headings
- generally, there are three spaces separating one column from the next
- there is one line of sample data shown
- the last column is **never** used
- text values are written left justified in their field width
- a data value too large to fit in its field width is truncated
- numeric values are written right justified in their field width.

## 10.4  Some Screen Functions

We want to be able to obtain a blank screen, to position the cursor anywhere on the screen, to draw vertical and horizontal lines and to draw boxes. Further, if we are not using a standard PC screen, then we might want to define the number of rows and columns to be used. Unfortunately, there is no standard library for controlling screen displays, so we have to either write our own or use the one supplied with our compiler. But first, let us look at a program which clears the screen, draws a box and then prints a simple message in the middle of the screen.

```
/* program 10.1 - clears the screen, draws a box,      */
/* positions the cursor.                               */


#include <stdio.h>
#include "screen.h"

void main(void)
{
   clearTheScreen();
   drawScreenFrame(10, 2, 60, 20);
   moveScreenCursorTo(35, 12);
   printf("Middle");
}
```

First, we include the contents of *screen.h*. The significance of the quotation marks surrounding *screen.h* is that the file is in the same directory as program 10.1. If *screen.h* was in the same directory as all the header files from the standard libraries, then you would replace the quotation marks with angle brackets, < and > – but this does depend on the C programming environment you are using. We shall examine the contents of *screen.h* later.

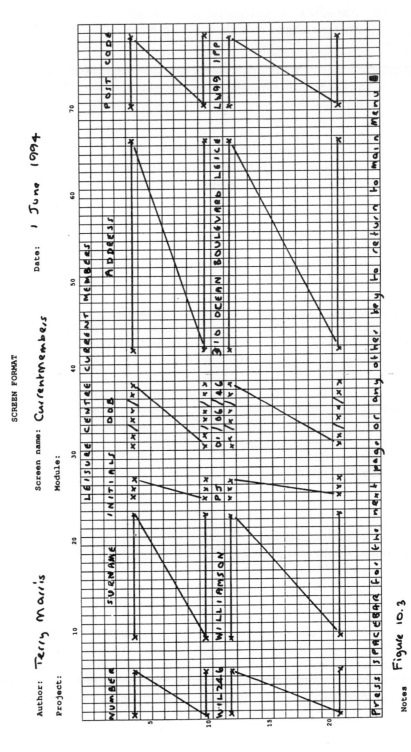

**Figure 10.3**

The line

```
clearTheScreen();
```

produces a blank screen and leaves the cursor in the top left-hand corner.

To draw a rectangle with its top left hand corner at column 10, row 2, of width 60 columns and height 20 rows we specify

```
drawScreenFrame(10, 2, 60, 20);
```

The format is

```
drawScreenFrame(column, row, width, height)
```

Finally, the line

```
moveScreenCursorTo(35, 12);
```

moves the cursor to column 35 row 12. So, the format is

```
moveScreenCursorTo(column, row);
```

If your C programming system comes complete with its own library of functions for clearing the screen, positioning the cursor and drawing lines and rectangles, then you should use these.

## 10.5   The Screen Header File

The file *screen.h* provides an interface between the program (program 10.1 for example) which uses the screen handling functions and the implementation of these functions. We shall look at them later. But for now let us examine some of the contents of *screen.h*.

```
/* screen.h - interface with screen handling functions. */

enum { lastScreenColumnNumber = 78, lastScreenRowNumber = 24 };

void clearTheScreen(void);
void moveScreenCursorTo(unsigned column, unsigned row);
void drawScreenFrame(unsigned column, unsigned row,
                     unsigned width, unsigned height);
```

*screen.h* contains an enumeration and a list of function templates.

Now, the size of a typical PC screen is 80 columns by 25 rows. The first row and the first column are both numbered zero. So, the last row would be numbered 24. We do not use the last column on the screen because, when the cursor reaches it, the cursor might either stay there or move to the beginning of the next line down – depending on which terminal you are using. If you are using a different sized screen, then you would need to change the last column and row numbers in the line

```
enum { lastScreenColumnNumber = 78,
                              lastScreenRowNumber = 24 };
```

to suit.
    We now state the specification of each function.

```
void clearTheScreen(void);
/* Clears the screen and leaves cursor in top left    */
/* hand corner.                                        */


void moveScreenCursorTo(unsigned column, unsigned row);
/* Moves cursor to coordinates (column, row).          */
/* Top left hand corner has coordinates (0, 0).        */
/* Pre-condition:  column <= lastScreenColumnNumber,   */
/*                 row <= lastScreenRowNumber           */
```

Evidently, we cannot move the cursor to a position outside the screen. So we place restrictions on the allowable values of column and row.

```
void drawScreenFrame(unsigned column, unsigned row,
                     unsigned width, unsigned height);
/* Draws a rectangular frame with top left hand        */
/* corner at coordinates (column, row), of width       */
/* columns wide and height rows high.                  */
/* Pre-condition: column + width <= lastScreenColumnNumber, */
/*                row + height <= lastScreenRowNumber,  */
```

Again, we cannot draw a box outside the dimensions of the screen.
    We need to specify how each of the functions is implemented. This is done in *screen.c*.

## 10.6  Implementation of Screen Handling Functions

The functions which actually perform the tasks of clearing the screen, positioning the cursor and drawing a rectangular frame are implemented in *screen.c*. The implementation is for a personal computer using DOS as its operating system.

```
/* screen.c - DOS implementation, uses ANSI codes. */
#include <stdio.h>
#include <stdlib.h>
#include "screen.h"

/* ASCII extended character set codes for frame      */
/* components.  topRight is top right hand corner.    */
/* hLine is a horizontal line element, ie a -.        */

enum { hLine = 196, vLine = 179, topRight = 191,
       botRight = 217, topLeft = 218, botLeft = 192 };


void moveCursor(unsigned x, unsigned y);
void drawFrame(unsigned x, unsigned y,
               unsigned w, unsigned h);


void clearTheScreen(void)
{
  printf("\033[2J");
}


void moveScreenCursorTo(unsigned col, unsigned row)
{
  if (col > lastScreenColumnNumber) {
    printf("moveScreenCursorTo: Column must not be more");
    printf(" than %u\n", lastScreenColumnNumber);
    exit(EXIT_FAILURE);
  }
  else if (row > lastScreenRowNumber) {
    printf("moveScreenCursorTo: Row must be not more");
    printf(" than %u\n", lastScreenRowNumber);
    exit(EXIT_FAILURE);
  }
  else
    moveCursor(col, row);
}

void moveCursor(unsigned x, unsigned y)
{
  printf("\033[%u;%uH", y + 1, x + 1);
}
```

```
void drawScreenFrame(unsigned col, unsigned row,
                          unsigned width, unsigned height)
{
  if (col + width > lastScreenColumnNumber) {
    printf("Frame: too wide to fit on the screen.\n");
    exit(EXIT_FAILURE);
  }
  else if (row + height > lastScreenRowNumber) {
    printf("Frame: too high to fit on the screen.\n");
    exit(EXIT_FAILURE);
  }
  else if ((width == 0) && (height == 0)) {
    printf("Frame: cannot print box with both zero length ");
    printf("and zero height.\n");
    exit(EXIT_FAILURE);
  }
  else
    drawFrame(col, row, width, height);
}


void drawFrame(unsigned x, unsigned y, unsigned w, unsigned h)
{
  unsigned col, row;

  moveCursor(x + 1, y);
  for (col = x + 1; col < x + w; col++)
    printf("%c", hLine);
  for (row = y + 1; row < y + h; row++) {
    moveCursor(x + w, row);  printf("%c", vLine);
  }
  for (row = y + 1; row < y + h; row++) {
    moveCursor(x, row);  printf("%c", vLine);
  }
  moveCursor(x + 1, y + h);
  if (w != 0)
    for (col = x; col < x + w - 1; col++)
      printf("%c", hLine);
  if ((w != 0) && (h != 0)) {
    moveCursor(x + w, y);
    printf("%c", topRight);
    moveCursor(x + w, y + h);
    printf("%c", botRight);
    moveCursor(x, y);
    printf("%c", topLeft);
```

```
      moveCursor(x, y + h);
      printf("%c", botLeft);
   }
}
```

The presence of the function prototypes

```
void moveCursor(unsigned x, unsigned y);
void drawFrame(unsigned x, unsigned y,
               unsigned w, unsigned h);
```

in *screen.c* specify that these functions are private to *screen.c* and cannot be accessed by any program or function outside *screen.c*.

*clearTheScreen* is implemented like this

```
void clearTheScreen(void)
{
   printf("\033[2J");
}
```

What is this *\033[2J*? It is the American National Standards Institute (ANSI) code which clears the screen and leaves the cursor in the top left-hand corner. This should have the same effect with different operating systems and different monitors provided the screen driver *ansi.sys* has been installed and loaded. This is achieved on a standard PC by including the line

```
DEVICE=C:\DOS\ANSI.SYS
```

in the system startup file, *config.sys* (assuming *ansi.sys* is in the DOS directory on drive C). (If you make a change to *config.sys*, remember to re-boot your computer so that the change may take effect.)

Similarly, an ANSI code is used to position the cursor in the function *moveCursor*.

```
void moveCursor(unsigned x, unsigned y)
{
   printf("\033[%u;%uH", y + 1, x + 1);
}
```

Details of these ANSI codes are usually found in the operating system handbook supplied with your computer.

*moveCursor* is called by *moveScreenCursorTo*. The purpose of *moveScreenCursorTo* is to act as a filter, allowing only valid row and column values to reach *moveCursor*. (If a monitor uses 25 rows and 80 columns for its display, what would happen if you asked the cursor to be positioned at column 81 row 26?)

Let us look at some of the lines in *drawFrame*. In *drawFrame* we find

```
for (col = x + 1; col < x + w; col++)
  printf("%c", hLine);
```

This is a short way of writing

```
col = x + 1;
while (col < x + w) {
  printf("%c", hLine);
  col++;
}
```

The *for...* loop construction has three control parts, each separated by semi-colons.

The first part, *col = x + 1*, is done once. This is the initialisation part.

The second part is the Boolean expression *col < x + w*. The loop body, in this case, the *printf* statement, is executed for as long as the Boolean expression remains *TRUE*. It corresponds to *while (boolean-expression)*.

The third part, *col++*, is executed at the end of every repetition. It ensures that, eventually, the Boolean expression becomes *FALSE*.

In the *printf* statement, *hLine* represents the horizontal line character in the extended ASCII table. The codes for the extended character set are usually defined in the operating system handbook supplied with your computer system.

### 10.7   The Linking Problem

You can compile a file such as screen.c to obtain screen.obj. You can compile a program such as prog101.c (that is, program 10.1) to obtain prog101.obj. How can these two object files be linked to create an executable program? The answer varies from one C programming system to another. Typically, you either include it as an argument to the linker on the operating system command line, or you create a project file.

An example of using the command line at the operating system prompt is

```
link prog101.obj screen.obj
```

An executable file named prog101.exe is created.

Typically, a project file lists the files to be compiled and linked. It is created with a text editor in the same way you create program text. A project file named prog101.prj might contain the two lines

```
screen.obj
prog101
```

This would instruct the C programming system to compile prog101.c, link prog101.obj with screen.obj and any other necessary libraries, and, since the project file is named prog101.prj, create the executable program named prog101.exe.  Of course, screen.obj must exist and the C programming system must know where to find it. If you are using an integrated programming development environment, you usually need to specify the project file name. Project files are not C files; so you cannot include C comments in them, for example.

If the implementation, *screen.c*, is changed in any way, then it must be re-compiled to create an up-to-date object file before you attempt to compile and link a program which uses it.

### Exercise 10.1

1 Try out program 10.1 on your computer system. If you wish to use the screen-handling functions supplied with your C programming system, then make the appropriate changes to the program. If you wish to use the functions supplied in screen.c, then screen.h and screen.c must exist on your system (you either type them in or get a copy from the disk supplied) and screen.c must be compiled (not run) before you compile and run program 10.1.
2 A horizontal line is a rectangle with zero height. A vertical line is a rectangle with zero width. Write a function to draw a noughts-and-crosses grid on the screen. Then complete a program which will record the moves made by two players in a noughts-and-crosses game.

### 10.8   Menus and Forms

Program 10.2 shown below displays a menu and inputs the user's choice.

```
/* program 10.2 - displays a menu, enters user's choice. */

#include <stdio.h>
#include <string.h>
#include "screen.h"

char choiceFromMenu(char menu[], char validChoices[]);
/* Displays menu.                                        */
/* Post-condition: returns a value from validChoices.    */

char mainMenu(void);
/* Displays menu.                                        */
/* Post-condition: returns a menu choice.                */


void main(void)
{
   char choice = mainMenu();
}
```

```
char choiceFromMenu(char menu[], char validChoices[])
{
  enum { false };

  char choice[BUFSIZ];
  int choiceIsOK = false;

  while (!choiceIsOK) {
    clearTheScreen();
    printf("%s", menu);
    gets(choice);
    choiceIsOK = ((strlen(choice) != 0) &&
              (strchr(validChoices, choice[0]) != NULL));
    if (!choiceIsOK) {
      moveScreenCursorTo(0, 24);
      printf("Your choice is not available - ");
     printf("press return then make another selection. ");
      gets(choice);
    }
  }
  return choice[0];
}


char mainMenu(void)
{
  char menu[] = "\n\n"
"                  SQUASH COURT BOOKINGS SYSTEM\n\n\n"
"                       BOOKINGS MENU\n\n"
"              1   Make a booking\n\n"
"              2   Cancel a booking\n\n"
"              3   Look up a booking\n\n"
"              4   Print a day's bookings\n\n"
"              5   Archive the day's bookings\n\n"
"              0   Exit from this menu\n\n\n"
"              Your choice? ";

  char validChoices[] = "0,1,2,3,4,5";

  return choiceFromMenu(menu, validChoices);

}
```

*main* calls *mainMenu*. *mainMenu* specifies the menu to be displayed, initialises *validChoices* and calls *choiceFromMenu*. *choiceFromMenu* repeatedly clears the screen, displays the menu, checks the choice input by the user and, if the choice is incorrect, informs the user on line 24 about what to do next. These steps are repeated until the choice entered is zero. The value returned by *mainMenu* can then be processed by *main*.

Now, to display the data entry form as shown in Figure 10.2 is straightforward. The problem is restricting the user's input to the designated spaces on the screen. When the user enters a surname for example, then it is possible for the user to overtype the following *Date of Birth* caption. What we need is a function which restricts the number of characters that can be entered by the user. Standard C does not provide a solution to this problem, but some C compiler vendors do. We write our own version of *gets* to do the job. Here is its specification.

```
char *screenStringRead(int width);
/* returns at most width characters entered at        */
/* the keyboard.                                       */
```

An example of a call to this function is

```
char *name = screenStringRead(10);
```

The user is allowed to enter at most ten characters to be stored in name. Here is its implementation.

```
char *screenStringRead(int width)
{
  enum { false, true };


  char *string;
  char charArray[BUFSIZ] = { '\0' };
  int i = 0;
  int done = false;
  int ch = characterRead();    /* See below for details */


  while (ch != EOF && !done) {
                    /* EOF - end of file character */
    switch (ch) {
    case '\0':           /* NULL character read, extended */
      characterRead();                /* code to follow. */
    case '\n':           /* Finish if return is pressed. */
    case '\r':
      done = true;
      break;
```

```
      case '\b':        /* Deal with destructive backspace. */
        if (i > 0) {
           printf("%c%c%c", '\b', ' ', '\b');
           i--;
        }
        break;

      default:
        if (isprint(ch)) {          /* if ch is printable */
           if (i < width) {     /* if there is still space */
              printf("%c", ch);           /* print it and */
              charArray[i] = ch;          /* store it. */
              i++;
           }
        }
        break;
     }
     if (!done)
        ch = characterRead();
  }
  charArray[i] = '\0';
  string = (char *)malloc(strlen(charArray) + 1);
  strcpy(string, charArray);
  return string;
}
```

We need to obtain a character from the keyboard and then decide whether it should be echoed to the screen. C does not provide such a function. So again we either use one provided with our C programming system or we write our own. We shall write our own. Here is its specification.

```
int characterRead(void);
/* Returns the next character from the keyboard without    */
/* echo to the screen and without holdup waiting for       */
/* return to be pressed.                                   */
```

Whichever way we implement this function, it will be non-standard; it will work with some C programming environments and not with others. This version uses the DOS operating system interface function, *bdos*, supplied with Borland Turbo C.

```
int characterRead(void)
{
   return (bdos(7, 0, 0) & 0x00ff);
}
```

The template for *bdos* is found in the Borland specific *dos* library. Most compiler vendors supply a library of functions which interface with the operating system. An explanation of how *bdos* works is beyond the scope of this book. The interested reader might like to see Bickerstaff, *System Software Tools* (Prentice-Hall, 1986), for further details.

We include the template for *screenStringRead* and *characterRead* in *screen.h* and the implementation of *screenStringRead* in *screen.c*.

## 10.9  Documentation

Screen format sheets are used to communicate designs for screen layouts, see Figures 10.1–10.3 for examples. The × signs are used to show regions designated for data input.

Incidentally, we avoid using the last column on the screen because we do not know in advance what the cursor will do when it reaches this column; it might either stay there or move to the beginning of the next line down.

## 10.10  Programming Principles

Know the intended user and how they work. In practice, this might involve doing their job for six months.

Have the user in mind when you design the interface between the program and its user.

Make use of what the compiler vendor has supplied to help you make your programs useable.

*Exercise 10.3*

1 Write a program which will display the entire form specified in Figure 10.3 and then accept input for each field at its appropriate place on the screen.

# 11

# Projects

## 11.1 Introduction

Most of us are required to complete a substantial programming project. Typically, this would involve writing a program to maintain a file. Either we are given a well-defined task to do or we choose one of our own.

## 11.2 Choosing a Subject

The project you choose should have sufficient scope to demonstrate analytical and design skills and your ability to use a wide range of programming techniques. Here are some ideas for a programming project.

1. Dating agency
2. Employment agency
3. Farming records
4. Plant nursery
5. Resource scheduling, e.g. rooms in a college
6. Hotel/holiday bookings
7. Airline reservation system
8. Squash court reservation system
9. Cashpoint machine simulation
10. Point-of-sale terminal
11. Specialised diets
12. Direct computer supplies mail order business
13. Labelling drugs dispensed by a pharmacy
14. Criminal investigation/enquiry system
15. Student records system
16. A simple spreadsheet
17. Forecasting crime
18. Spell-checker

**19** Editor (a simple word processor)
**20** Classification system, e.g. books in a library
**21** Bird identification system
**22** A program style checker
**23** A language translator, e.g. English into French
**24** Books sent on approval recording system
**25** Advertising hoardings control system
**26** Immigration control
**27** Car/van/boat/coach hire
**28** Computer printer paper stock control and automatic re-ordering system
**29** Evening course enquiries and booking system at a college
**30** City marathon entries
**31** College library services
**32** Hospital/dental/doctor records and automatic patient recall system
**33** Theatre seat reservations
**34** Taxi business – private hire
**35** Time accounting – preparation of bill to repair, say, electrical goods
**36** Time accounting in a solicitor's/accountant's office
**37** Credit card accounting for a department store
**38** Scheduling music exams for a school of music
**39** Video hire company
**40** Horse trials reservations, entries and results system
**41** Recreation parks maintenance for a city council
**42** Costing the manufacture of goods such as PCs/aAmplifiers/CD players
**43** Motor vehicle maintenance schedule for a haulage/bus company
**44** Tracking parcels in transit – parcel carrying company
**45** Software packages used by a college/company
**46** Personnel management in a company manufacturing plastic dinosaurs
**47** Payroll for a medium-sized knitwear company
**48** Objects, etc. in a city museum
**49** Paintings, etc. in a city art gallery
**50** Vet's patients records system
**51** Piano tuner clients database and automatic reminder system
**52** Garage – customer vehicles maintenance/repair and service reminder
**53** Estate agents
**54** Parking-ticket fine repayments system
**55** Prison service records
**56** Leisure centre membership
**57** Insurance company policies and pensions
**58** Car insurance quotation and brokerage system
**59** Skip hire
**60** Mortgage loans vetting system

The project you choose should be non-trivial, of interest to you and approved by your programming supervisor.

## 11.3 The Project Report

A project is usually evaluated on the basis of a project report together with a demonstration of the working program (or programs).

Your report must be word processed and sectioned.

If a marking scheme is supplied, then you should constantly bear it in mind when you write up your project report. A useful technique is to provide a heading for each component of the marking scheme and then ensure that you include the required details under each heading.

If the marking scheme is not so detailed, then consider providing each of the following sections in your project report.

### 11.3.1 Contents Page

Each page of the project report should be numbered. The first page, a contents page, lists the main sections of the project report together with their page numbers.

### 11.3.2 Summary

Although this section is the second one to appear in the report, it is usually written last. This section contains an outline of your project. It comprises the main points such as the subject chosen, what you set out to do and what you actually achieved. The summary should take up no more than one side of paper.

### 11.3.3 System Description

A program does not exist in isolation. It is usually a very small part of a much wider data processing system. In this section, you should describe the entire data processing system in as much detail as possible. For example, suppose your project features a video hire shop, then this section should describe in detail

- how individual copies of each video are identified
- the order in which the videos are placed on the shelves
- whether a person has to be a member before they can take a video out
- how a person selects a video
- how a person's choice is recorded
- how an employee knows where each copy of each video is currently located
- what happens when a video is returned on time
- what happens when a video is returned late
- how an employee knows when a video has not been returned
- what happens when a booked out video is lost or stolen
- what happens when a video becomes "worn out"
- how theft of videos is detected
- how the manager knows what new video titles are available
- how the manager decides what new videos to acquire
- what happens when new videos arrive in the shop

- how the manager determines what the day's money receipts should be
- how the manager knows which titles or categories are most/least popular
- how the manager determines whether the business is making a profit
- how cash flow for each month is predicted
- how predicted cash flow is compared with actual cash flow.

If possible, you should work (free of charge?) in a video hire shop to gain first-hand experience of how such as shop is actually run.

However, it is not usually possible to obtain experience in the subject of your choice. For example if you decide to do a project on immigration control, then it is unlikely that you will be allowed to see what goes on behind the scenes, and they will not tell you what happens either. In such cases, you will have to use your imagination. But at least you should be able to obtain application forms and copies of rules which are available to the general public.

You should obtain any brochures and forms relevant to your project and do as much research as you reasonably can in the time you have got.

### 11.3.4  Program Description

You should choose just a small part of the data processing system described in section 11.3.3 and describe what you want your program (or programs) to do.

### 11.3.5  Report Specifications

Many projects will print the contents of a file in the form of a report. In this section, you specify using printer format sheets, the layout of each report.

### 11.3.6  The User Interface

Screen format sheets which specify the screens the user will see and use should be in this section. Further, you should describe and justify your designs for the user interface.

### 11.3.7  Data Dictionaries

The structure and content of every file should be explained in this section. For each file you should specify its name, size, purpose, access mode and record name. For each record you should list, specify and explain each field. Data dictionary forms would be useful here.

### 11.3.8  Program Structure Charts

Program structure charts should show, for each program, the main functions and the data types of their arguments and return values. No structure chart should fill more than one side of normal size paper. If a structure chart cannot be fitted comfortably on one side of paper, then each of its main parts should be expanded on a second sheet.

For example, suppose a menu function called seven other functions (and each of these functions themselves called other functions) then one page would contain just the menu function together with the seven functions; another page would feature just one of these seven functions together with the functions it calls. And so on.

Remember to draw your structure charts large and neat. A sharp pencil used throughout, for lines, arrows and captions, is perhaps best.

### 11.3.9   Test Plans

Your test plans should

- specify how every choice in every menu is to be tested
- specify the contents of each file
- list the changes to be made to each file

together with any other values required to thoroughly test your program or programs.

### 11.3.10   Evaluation of Design

A colleague should examine your designs and just list any faults he or she thinks it contains. Nothing more. Then you have the choice of either ignoring them, or doing nothing about them except to mention them in your own evaluation of your project or re-designing your project. The aim here is to at least be aware of any shortcomings in your designs.

### 11.3.11   Program Listings

Your program listings **must** be separated into single sheets. They should be clean, that is, free of any handwritten changes or comments. Of course, the programs should compile without error.

### 11.3.12   Program Runs

Here, you should provide evidence of your program running successfully. This evidence may take the form of printed output from of file contents or, where there is no screen formatting, program runs can be echoed to the printer. Hardcopy **must** be annotated, titled and explained by hand.

Photographs of your formatted screen displays are useful.

### 11.3.13   Test Logs

Your test logs should be an honest account of all your program runs, even the failures.

### 11.3.14   User Instructions

The user wants to know how to run your program, not how to use the editor and compiler! The user needs to know what files must be on what disks and in which directories. The user wants to know what happens when the program is running and what to do in the event of program failure. To test the effectiveness of your user instructions, consider inviting a non-computer person to run your program from your written instructions alone, without any verbal help from yourself.

### 11.3.15 Evaluation of Implementation

A colleague should run your program and list its shortcomings. The purpose here is just to detect errors.

### 11.3.16 Evaluation and Review

In this section you look back over what you have done and compare what you have achieved with what you set out to do.

You discuss any shortcomings of your programs (such as file only contains 100 records, in a real situation, 10,000 records would be held; or the user is not allowed to input the date any reasonable format; or program crashes when a very large number is input; or in the real situation, there would be multi-user access to the files).

Finally, you describe any improvements and enhancements you could make to your project.

## 11.4  Size and Complexity

As your programs become larger, so they become more complex and more difficult to design and write. So, we need strategies for dealing with size and managing complexity.

We already split programs up into functions, each of which does one small specific task. In Chapter 10 we saw how to separate a set of related functions (for example, screen.c) from programs which use them. Now we see how one program may call another.

First, we write and run *prog2* so that *prog2.exe* is created.

```
/* prog2.c */
#include <stdio.h>
void main(void)
{
   printf("Inside prog2 \n");
}
```

Then we write *prog1* which calls *prog2*.

```
/* prog1.c - calls prog2. */
#include <stdio.h>
#include <stdlib.h>
```

```
void main(void)
{
  printf("Inside prog1 \n");
  system("prog2");
  printf("Back inside prog1");
}
```

When *prog1* is run

```
Inside prog1
Inside prog2
Back inside prog1
```

is displayed.

The line

```
system("prog2");
```

says go and do program *prog2* and then return. *system* is defined in *stdlib*.

Calls to *system* cannot usually be nested. For example, if *system* is used to call *prog2* which itself uses *system* to call *prog3*, then the method may not work as expected.

Files which are open may need to be closed before a call to *system* is made.

A file can be used to communicate values between a program and the program which calls it.

Well, how can all this help you in practice? *prog1* could contain your main menu. Then, *prog2* could be the program which prints out a report of the contents of a file. If this report contains headings, page numbers and summary totals on each page, then the program is likely to run into several hundred lines. In a similar way, *prog1* could call other programs, each of which performs a specific task such as adding a new record to a file or amending a record already in a file.

## 11.5  Date and Time

Many programs deal with dates and times. The next program obtains the date and time from the computer system and displays them on the screen.

```
/* program 11.3 - gets date and time from the        */
/* operating system (if available) and displays them. */
#include <stdio.h>
#include <time.h>
```

```
void main(void)
{
    time_t systemTime;

    if (time(&systemTime) == -1)
        printf("Time not available from the system.\n");
    else
        printf(ctime(&systemTime));
}
```

An example of what is shown on the screen when the program is run is

```
Fri Jul 22 08:44:02 1994
```

The line

```
time_t systemTime;
```

declares the variable *systemTime* to be of type *time-t*. *time-t* is defined in *time.h*. Variables of type *time-t* contain the date and time in an implementation defined manner.

The *time* function reads the current date and time from the operating system and stores it in a variable of type *time_t* – if it can. If *time* fails to read the current date and time, it returns *-1* cast to type *time_t*.

The function *ctime* displays a date and time held in a variable of type *time_t*.

Program 11.4 again obtains the date and time from the operating system, but this time makes the data available in a pre-defined structure.

```
/* program 11.4 - gets date and time from the operating */
/*                system, displays date in the format    */
/*                weekDay, dayInMonth, monthName, year.   */
/*                eg Friday 22 July 1994.                 */
#include <stdio.h>
#include <time.h>

char *weekDay[] = { "Sunday", "Monday", "Tuesday",
                    "Wednesday", "Thursday", "Friday",
                    "Saturday" };

char *month[] = { "January", "February", "March", "April",
                  "May","June", "July", "August", "September",
                  "October", "November", "December" };
```

```
void main(void)
{
    time_t systemTime;
    struct tm *pTime;
    time(&systemTime);
    pTime = localtime(&systemTime);
    printf("%s %d %s %d",
            weekDay[pTime->tm_wday], pTime->tm_mday,
            month[pTime->tm_mon], 1900 + pTime->tm_year);
}
```

The line pTime = localtime(&systemTime); converts date and time held in *time_t* format into the structure *tm*. *tm* contains the following fields

```
int tm_sec          second (0..59)
int tm_min          minute (0..59)
int tm_hour         hour (0..23), 0 == midnight
int tm_mday         day of the month (1..31)
int tm_mon          month (0..11), 0 == January
int tm_year         year since 1900
int tm_wday         day of the week (0..6), 0 == Sunday
int tm_yday         day of the year (0..366)
```

The function *localtime* reads the date and time, as returned by the function *time* for example, uses the date and time to initialise a variable of type *tm*, and then returns a pointer to the variable.

The line struct tm *pTime; defines a variable named *pTime* which is a pointer to a structure of type *struct tm*.

Once you have a date broken down into the format of the structure *tm* you are free to manipulate it as you please.

The types *time_t* and *tm* and the functions *time*, *ctime* and *localtime* are all specified in *time.h*.

## 11.6  Conclusion

If you have completed several projects in the past, then you will have noticed that

- projects always take longer than you think they will
- computers always crash at the worst possible moment
- the disk which contains the only copy of your project always becomes corrupt or lost or stolen in the last week.

So, always be prepared for the worst possible disaster to happen.

# Appendix A: Language Summary

## A.1 Introduction

In this appendix we review the basic features of the language. The standard libraries are covered in Appendix B.

## A.2 Comments

Comments are introduced with /* and terminated with */. Comments cannot be nested and they cannot occur within string literals.

## A.2 Identifiers

Identifiers are names for objects such as keywords, functions, variables and constant values. An identifier must

- begin with a letter
- contain only letters and digits and underscores

An upper-case letter is not the same as its lower-case version. Usually, identifiers may be any length but the first 31 characters are significant. However the operating system may impose further restrictions on external identifiers such as those used for disk file names.

## A.3 Keywords

The following identifiers are reserved for keywords.

```
auto        double      int         struct
break       else        long        switch
case        enum        register    typedef
char        extern      return      union

const       float       short       unsigned
continue    for         signed      void
default     goto        sizeof      volatile
defined     if          static      while
do
```

These keywords must be used according to their definition; they cannot be used in any other way.

### A.4 Constants

An integer constant is a sequence of digits. An integer constant may be suffixed with *U* (for *unsigned*), *L* (for *long*) or *UL* (for *unsigned long*). The letters *u* and *l* serve the same purpose. An integer constant without a suffix is an ordinary *int* value. Examples of integer constants are

```
76, 0U, -47309L, 234567UL
```

A character constant is one (or more) characters enclosed within single quotes. For example, *'a', 'Z'*. A single character is translated into its number equivalent at runtime. Character constants containing two characters include

```
\n  newline              \\  the backslash itself
\b  backspace            \?  the question mark
\r  return               \'  the single quote
\a  alert or bell        \"  the double quote
```

So, even though '\n' looks like two characters, it represents just one – the *newline* character.

A *float* constant is a number with a decimal point; it has the suffix *F* (or *f*) for *float* or *L* (or *l*) for *long double*. A *float* value without a suffix is a *double*.

```
3.1416F,    193457.320234L, 23.007
```

The identifiers in an enumeration represent constant values of type *int*.

```
enum {Sunday,Monday,Tuesday,Wednesday,Thursday,
                            Friday,Saturday };
```

Here, *Sunday* has the value *0*, *Monday* the value *1*, *Tuesday 2*, and so on.

### A.5 String Literals

A string literal (also known as a string constant) is a sequence of characters enclosed by double quotes. The last character, automatically placed there by the compiler, is the end-of-string character, \0. A string literal has type array of *char* and storage class *static*.

```
char message[] = "Program halted - unexpected error.";
```

Adjacent string literals are concatenated into a single string literal. For example the six string literals listed here

```
char menu[] = "Main menu.\n";
               "1   New\n";
               "2   Open\n";
               "3   Close\n";
               "9   Quit\n";
               "Choice? ";
```

are automatically joined into one long one, complete with the terminating *NULL* character, and stored in *menu*.

## A.6  Storage Class

Storage classes include *auto* and *static*. A storage class describes how an object is to be stored in memory.

Variables of storage class *auto* are created every time the block in which they are declared is entered, and are destroyed every time the block is exited. This is the default storage class.

Variables of storage class *static* are created the first time the block in which they are defined is entered and remain in existence until program execution terminates.

```
void function(void)
{
   auto int number;
/* auto is not explicitly required.                */
/* Created anew on entry to the function.           */
/* Destroyed on exit from the function.             */
   static int state;
/* Persists between function calls.                 */
   ...
}
```

## A.7  Basic Types

The fundamental types include

| | |
|---|---|
| char | *a character* |
| int | *an integer* |
| float | *a single precision floating point number* |
| double | *a double precision floating point number* |
| short | *short int* |
| long | *long int* |
| unsigned | *unsigned int* |
| unsigned long | *unsigned long int* |
| void | *the empty type has no values* |

## A.8 The Usual Arithmetic Conversions

The usual arithmetic conversions ensure that both operands are of the same type before an arithmetic process takes place. In general, if two operands have different types then the operand with the "lower" type is promoted to the same type as the other operand. The following table lists the types in order.

```
long double      highest type
double
float

unsigned long
long
unsigned
int
short
char             lowest type
```

Conversions between signed and unsigned values depend on the implementation. For example, suppose one operand is *long* and the other is *unsigned*: if the *long* type can represent all the *unsigned int* values, then the *unsigned* operand is converted to *long*, otherwise, both are converted to *unsigned long*. The result of a calculation which involves both *signed* and *unsigned* values should be carefully checked.

## A.9 Promotion

On assignment, a value is automatically promoted to a higher type if necessary. The hierarchy of types is shown in section A.8. It is perhaps best to explicitly promote values with a cast operator. For example

```
(double) intValue;
```

converts the contents of *intValue* into one of type *double*. Demoting a value to one of a lower type via casts should be done with care.

A pointer may be converted (via a cast) to *void* * and back again without loss of information.

## A.10 The Operators

An operator specifies a process to be applied to one or two operands. The C operators include

```
!           not
!=          compare two numbers for inequality
#           substitute pre-processor token
```

| | |
|---|---|
| % | *modulus, i.e. remainder after dividing one number by another* |
| && | *logical and* |
| ( ) | *cast operators* |
| * | *multiply two numbers* |
| + | *add two numbers* |
| ++ | *increment a number by one* |
| , | *work out the value of an expression* |
| – | *subtract one number from another* |
| -- | *decrement a number by one* |
| -> | *select a member of (a pointer to) a structure* |
| . | *select a member of a structure* |
| / | *divide one number by another* |
| < | *less than* |
| <= | *less than (or equal to)* |
| = | *assignment* |
| == | *equality* |
| > | *greater than* |
| >= | *greater than (or equal to)* |
| [] | *array subscript* |
| defined | *check if a macro has been defined* |
| sizof | *size of operand in bytes* |
| \|\| | *logical or* |

Precedence is the default order in which the operators in an expression are evaluated. Precedence is always overridden by ( ). The precedence of the operators is shown in the following table; operators higher up in the table have a higher precedence than those lower down.

| Operator | | | | | | Associativity |
|---|---|---|---|---|---|---|
| ( ) | [] | -> | . | | | *left to right* |
| ! | ++ | -- | (type)* | & | sizeof | *right to left* |
| * | / | % | | | | *left to right* |
| + | – | | | | | *left to right* |
| < | <= | > | >= | | | *left to right* |
| == | != | | | | | *left to right* |
| && | | | | | | *left to right* |
| \|\| | | | | | | *left to right* |
| = | | | | | | *right to left* |
| , | | | | | | *left to right* |

Within a given level of precedence, associativity describes the direction of evaluation. In the expression

```
while (c = 'a' != EOF)
```

*!=* has higher precedence than *=* and so the test *!=* is done before the assignment and
*c* is assigned either TRUE (1) or FALSE (0) depending on whether *'a'* is not equal to
*EOF*.
   In

```
while ((c = 'a') != EOF)
```

the *( )* has the highest precedence of all and so *c* is assigned the character *'a'* before
it is tested for inequality with *EOF*.

## A.11  Function Calls

A function call is an expression which involves a function name together with a pair
of braces. The braces may either contain nothing or a list of expressions known as
arguments. A copy of each argument value is passed, by the function call, to a
corresponding function parameter.

```
returnedValue = function(argument-1, argument-2, ... argument-n);
```

A function may change its parameter values without any affect whatsoever on any
argument variables. However, a function can indirectly change the contents of a
variable if it is handed a pointer to the variable.
   Both the arguments in a function call and the parameters in a parameter list must
match (usually) one for one the parameters declared in the function prototype.
   The order in which a functions parameter expressions are evaluated is not defined.
So, for example, if two functions are used as arguments, then there is no knowing which
function will be executed first.

```
returnedValue = functionName(function-1(argList-1),
                             function-2(argList-2))
```

The value returned by a function may either be ignored or used.

## A.12  Increment and Decrement Operators

The increment-by-one operator is *++* and the decrement-by-one operator is *--*. They
can either precede (prefix) or follow (postfix) an integer variable.
   *++i* and *i++* both have the same affect – to increase the value stored in *i* by one. But,
in the prefix version, *i* is incremented before it is used in an expression and, in the postfix
version, *i* is incremented after it is used. For example, if *numbers* is an array of *int* and

```
int i = 2;

printf("%d", numbers[++i]);   /* increment i then print. */
printf("%d", numbers[i++];    /* print then increment i. */
```

## A.13   The Address Operator

The address operator, &, returns the address of its operand. The operand must be a variable (or a function). The result is a pointer to the variable (or function).

```
int number = 2;
int *pointerToNumber = &number;  /* address of number  */
                                 /* is assigned to     */
                                 /* pointerToNumber.   */
```

## A.14   The Indirection Operator

The indirection operator, *, returns the value stored in the variable pointed to by its operand.

```
int number = 2;
int *pointerToNumber = &number;  /* pointerToNumber    */
                                 /* contains the       */
                                 /* address of number. */
*pointerToNumber == 2;
```

(The indirection operator may also return the function to which its operand points.)

## A.15   The Array Subscript Operator

An array type is a sequence of adjacent indexed storage locations all of which hold values of the same type. For example

```
char letters[12] = "Catastrophe";
```

defines an array named *letters* of size 12 elements, each element of which contains a single value of type *char*.

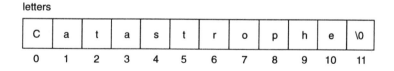

Arrays are always indexed from zero upwards. Each element is referenced by its index. For example,

```
letters[4] == 's';
```

Each element of an array can itself be an array. For example

```
char words[5][12];
```

defines a two-dimensional array named *words* which can up to store five lines each up to 12 characters long.

words

| | 0 | 1 | 2 | 3 | 4 | 5 | 6 | 7 | 8 | 9 | 10 | 11 |
|---|---|---|---|---|---|---|---|---|---|---|---|---|
| 0 | C | a | t | a | s | t | r | o | p | h | e | \0 |
| 1 | t | h | e | | c | a | t | \0 | | | | |
| 2 | i | s | | a | s | l | e | e | p | \0 | | |
| 3 | o | n | | t | h | e | \0 | | | | | |
| 4 | m | a | t | . | \0 | | | | | | | |
| | 0 | 1 | 2 | 3 | 4 | 5 | 6 | 7 | 8 | 9 | 10 | 11 |

To reference a particular element, the row index is given first. For example

```
words[2][5]  ==  'l'
```

## A.16   The Logical Not Operator

The logical not operator is denoted by *!*. Its operand must either be an arithmetic type or a pointer. It returns one (true) if if its operand is equal to zero (false), otherwise it return zero.

```
int n = 5;

!(n == 2) == 0;   /* false */
```

## A.17   The Sizeof Operator

The *sizeof* operator returns the number of bytes required to store a value of its operand type.

```
sizeof(char) == 1
```

```
sizeof(arrayType)  ==  number of bytes in the array
```

```
sizeof(structureType)  ==  number of bytes in the structure
```

## A.18  Casts

A cast causes a temporary change in the type of an expression to the type enclosed within brackets. For example

```
int intValue;
...
(double)intValue;
```

converts *intValue* to a value of type *double*.

## A.19  The Arithmetic Operators

The arithmetic operators are

| | | |
|---|---|---|
| * | multiplication | both operands must be arithmetic types, e.g. *int* or double |
| / | quotient | both operands must be arithmetic types. The second operand must not be zero |
| % | remainder | both operands must be integer types only. The second operand must not be zero. The result is not defined if either operand is negative. |
| + | addition | |
| − | subtraction | |

## A.20  The Relational Operators

The relational operators are

| | |
|---|---|
| < | less than |
| <= | less than or equal to |
| == | equal to |
| != | not equal to |
| >= | greater than or equal to |
| > | greater than |

The expression *operand-1 relational-operator operand-2* returns either one (true) or zero (false).

```
(5 > 3) == 1;  /* true */
(5 < 3) == 0;  /* false */
```

### A.21   The Logical Operators

The logical operators are && (logical and) and ∥ (logical or).

*(A && B)*   returns one (true) if both *A* and *B* are one (true) otherwise returns zero (false). Evaluation is always from left to right and halts as soon as the result is known.

*(A ∥ B)*   returns one (true) if either one of A or B is zero (false), otherwise returns zero (false). Evaluation is always from left to right.

For example,

```
(5 > 3) && (5 < 3) == 0;
          /* 5 greater than 3 and at the same time 5 < 3 */
  true          false          /* - false. */
```
   *true*          *false*

```
(5 > 3) && (3 > 1) == 1; /* true */
  true          true
```

```
(5 > 3) || (5 < 3) == 1; /* either 5 > 3 or 5 < 3 - true.*/
  true          false
```

```
(5 < 3) || (3 < 1) == 0;   /* false */
  false         false
```

### A.22   The Assignment Operators

The assignment operators include

```
 =  *=  /=  %=  +=  -=
```

The first (left) operand must be a modifiable item such as a variable or a structure. It must not be a const or an array or a function.
   An expression such as

```
m *= n
```

is equivalent to

```
m = m * n
```

### A.23   The Comma Operator

A pair of expressions separated by a comma are evaluated from left to right. For example

```
int n = 2, n++;
```

leaves *n* containing *3*.

## A.24   Structure-type Declarations

A structure consists of a collection of named objects called members. Each member has an identifier and a type. A structure declaration begins with the keyword *struct*. The declaration

```
typedef struct {
   char name[30];
   char payrollNumber[10];
   double annualSalary;
} Employee;
```

defines the *struct* type *Employee*. Variables of this type, as well as pointers to it, can be defined.

```
Employee employee;
Employee *pointerToEmployee;
```

The . member selector operator is used to refer to the contents of a particular member within a structure.

```
employee.salary.
```

If a pointer to a structure is involved, the offset operator ->is used to access a particular member.

```
pointerToEmployee->salary
```

## A.25   Enumerations

An enumeration is a list of identifiers which represent constants of type *int*. The values 0, 1, 2, ... are automatically assigned to each identifier as written from left to right. However, if an identifier is assigned an explicit value, then subsequent identifiers are automatically assigned values in sequence from that value onwards.

```
enum { Sunday,Monday,Tuesday,Wednesday,Thursday,Friday,Saturday };
```

assigns *0* to *Sunday*, *1* to *Monday*, *2* to *Tuesday*, ...

```
enum { lastIndex = 5, arraySize }
```

assigns *5* to *lastIndex* and *6* to *arraySize*.


## A.26   Declarations

Declarations have the format *type identifier*. Examples of declarations include

```
int number;           /* integer number */

int numbers[];        /* array of integers */

int *number;          /* pointer to integer */

int *numbers[];       /* array of pointers to integers */

const int n = 5;      /* integer constant - value cannot */
                      /* be changed during */
                      /* program execution. */
```


## A.27   Function Declarations

A function declaration announces a function's signature, that is, its return type, name and the number and type of its parameters. For example

```
int strcpy(char *destination, const char *source);
```

declares a function named *strcpy*. *strcpy* returns an *int* and has two parameters. The first parameter, named *destination*, is a pointer to *char*. The second parameter is a pointer to *const*ant *char*; this means that the sequence of characters pointed to by *source* cannot be changed by the function.


## A.28   Initialisation

Variables may be assigned their initial values at their point of declaration. Examples are

```
int number = 0;
unsigned long number = 0UL;

int *pointerToNumber = &number;
```

```
typedef struct {
  char name[30];
  char payrollNumber[10];
  double annualSalary;
} Employee;

Employee nullEmployee = { " ", " ", 0.00 };
                                /* each member is filled */


int days[] = { 0, 31, 28, 31, 30, 31, 30, 31, 31, 30,
              31, 30, 31 };
              /* size of array automatically computed */
              /* from the number of initialisers.     */


int numbers[5] = { 0, 0, 0, 0, 0 };
                        /* 0 is stored in each element */

char fatalErrorMessage[] =
              "Program halted - unexpected problem\n";
/* one character is stored in each successive location. */
```

A two-dimensional array might be initialised like this.

```
int studentsInYear[2][5] = { { 25, 17, 30, 25, 25 },
                             { 90, 91, 92, 93, 94 } }
```

To initialise a pointer to a structure, storage must first be allocated with *malloc*.

```
typedef   struct {
  char name[30];
  char payrollNumber[10];
  double annualSalary;
} Employee;

Employee *pointerToEmployee =
                    (Employee *)malloc(sizeof(Employee));
```

A pointer **must** be initialised with the address of an appropriate variable before it is dereferenced, that is, before an attempt is made to retrieve from, or write to, the location whose address is stored in the pointer, otherwise garbage may be retrieved or the contents of an arbitrary location in memory may be overwritten (which is disastrous if that location contains a part of the operating system).

### A.29   Typedef

*typedef* provides a new name for an existing type. For example

```
typedef enum { false, true } Boolean;
```

Here, the *enum { false, true }* is named *Boolean*. Hence we can declare *Boolean* variables thus

```
Boolean valueIsValid;
```

### A.30   Statements

Statements include assignments and function calls.

A compound statement comprises a sequence of statements enclosed within braces *{* and *}*. A compound statement may be used wherever a statement would be used.

### A.31   Selections

A selection statement transfers control. There are several forms.

*if (expression)*
  *statement*

*if (expression)*
  *statement-1*
*else*
  *statement-2*

*switch (expression)*
  *statement*

For example

```
if (cannotOpenFile) {
   printf("Program halted - cannot open the file.\n");
   exit(EXIT_FAILURE);
}
```

The *printf* and *exit* statements are executed only if *cannotOpenFile* is true, that is, only if *cannotOpenFile == 1*.

```
if (isFinished)
   fclose(file);
```

```
else
   fread(&record, sizeof(RecordStructure), 1 file);
```

The *fclose* statement is executed only if *isFinished* is true. However, if *isFinished* is not true, then *fread* is executed. Either *fclose* or *fread* is selected for execution.

The *switch* statement causes transfer of control to one or several case-labelled statements depending on value of expression. Only one *default* label is allowed per *switch* statement. *switch* statements may be nested.

```
switch (day) {
case 1: case 21:
case 31: printf("st");
   break;
case 2: case 22: printf("nd");
   break;
case 3: case 23: printf("rd");
   break;
default: printf("th");
   break;
}
```

When the *switch* statement is executed, *day* is evaluated. If its value is *1, 21* or *31*, *printf("st")* is selected for execution; if its value is *2* or *22, printf("nd")*; is selected; if its value is *3* or *23, printf("rd")* is selected. But if the value of day is neither *1, 21, 22, 23, 31, 2* nor *3*, the *default* case is executed and *printf("th")* is selected.

Once a *case* has been selected for execution, the following cases are also executed – unless control is transferred by a statement such as *break* or *exit* or *return*.

### A.32  Iteration

An iteration statement controls the number of times a statement is executed. One form is

*while (expression)*
 *statement*

For example

```
while (!feof(file)) {
   printRecord(record);
   fread(&record, sizeof(RecordStructure), 1, file);
}
```

For as long as *feof(file)* is not true, execute the *printRecord* and *fread* statements. It is possible that no iterations are made at all: if *feof(file)* is initially true, then the *printRecord* and *fread* statements are never executed.

Another form is

> *for (expression-1; expression-2; expression-3)*
>   *statement*

*expression-1*, *2* and *3* are optional.

```
for (i = 0; i <= lastIndex; i++)
    printf("%d\n", intArray[i]);
```

expression-1 *(i = 0)* corresponds to an initialisation stage. expression-2 *(i <= lastIndex)* is the expression which controls whether statement *(printf("%d\n", intArray[i]);)* is executed; it corresponds to while (expression). expression-3 *(i++)* corresponds to a re-initialisation stage; it is executed once at the end of every repetition.

## A.33   Unconditional Transfer of Control

The unconditional transfer of control statements include *break* and *return*.

*break* may appear only in an iteration or a switch – it terminates execution of the smallest enclosing statement.

*return* causes an immediate exit from a function, returning control to its caller. When return is followed by expression, the value is returned to the caller. Falling off the end of a function is equivalent to returning without a value.

## A.34   Function Definitions

A function definition is made up of a function declarator (i.e. function heading) together with a function body. A function declarator must match its prototype declaration. An array passed as a value to a function parameter is automatically converted to a pointer.

A function body usually comprises variable definitions together with a sequence of statements.

```
int strcpy(char *destination, const char *source)
{
    int n = 0;

    while ((*destination = *source) != '\0') {
        destination++;                              function
        source++;                                   body
        n++;
    }
    return n;
}
```

## A.35  Scope

The scope of an identifer is that part of a program in which the named object may be used.

```
/* program 12.1 - demonstrates scope. */

#include <stdio.h>

void function1(int prototypeParameter);

int globalVariable = 10;


void main(void)
{
   int localVariable = 2;

   function1(localVariable);
}


void function1(int parameterVariable)
{
   int localVariable;
            /* no conflict with localVariable in main. */

   for (localVariable = 0; localVariable < 5;
                          localVariable++) {
     int blockVariable = localVariable * parameterVariable;
     printf("%d ", blockVariable);
   }
   printf("%d\n", globalVariable);
}
```

When run, the program prints

```
0 2 4 6 8 10
```

on the screen.

The prototype parameter is recognised only within the prototype itself; its scope is the function prototype. Since it is not visible outside the prototype, prototype parameter identifiers are used only for documentation purposes.

A global variable may be used throughout the entire program file. Any function within the program file can access, modify and use the global variable. A global variable identifier has scope over the entire program file, from the point it is declared onwards.

However, if a local variable has the same identifier as a global variable, then it "masks" the global variable and any references to the identifier in the function refer to the local variable.

A local variable (including parameter variables) may be used only by the function in which it is declared. Local and parameter variable identifiers have scope confined to the function in which they are declared.

A block variable may be use only within the block (delimited by { and }) in which it is declared. An identifier with block scope is not visible outside the block in which it is declared. Again, a block variable "hides" a function variable with the same identifier.

Identical identifiers may be used without conflict providing their scopes are disjoint (that is, separate).

### A.36   The Pre-processor

The pre-processor performs tasks such as text substitution and file inclusion before translation takes place from C text (that is, C source code) into C object code. Instructions to the pre-processor, known as pre-processor directives, begin with #. Each directive must be written on a line of its own.

```
#define maxSize 100
```

replaces all occurrences of *maxSize* in a program file with *100* – except in comments and in quoted string literals.

```
#include <stdio.h>
#include "header.h"
```

includes the entire contents of *stdio.h* and *header.h* in the program file before compilation takes place. The angle brackets usually indicates that the file to be included is in the C system directory. The quotation marks usually indicates that the file to be included is in the same directory as the program text file.

It would be an error to include the same text more than one in the same program file. So, header files should contain something like

```
#if !defined
  #define headerFileIncluded
/* contents of header file go here. */
#endif
```

On the first inclusion of the header file, *headerFileIncluded* is not defined. So, it is defined and the text up to the next *#endif* is included. On any subsequent inclusion, *headerFileIncluded* has already been defined and so the text up to the next *#endif* is not included.

## A.37  Line Splicing

The continuation character, \, may be used to continue a statement on to the next line.

# Appendix B: Standard Library Summary

## B.1  Introduction

C is supported by a standard collection of constants and functions to manage, for example, memory, arrays of char (i.e. strings) and files. The constants and functions are grouped in library files. The library files together form the standard library. The most commonly used constants and functions are described in this appendix.

## B.2  The Standard Libraries

Table B.1 lists the standard libraries.

**Table B.1**   The standard libraries

| Library | Description |
| --- | --- |
| assert | diagnostic – check assertions at run-time |
| ctype | character processing |
| errno | error handling |
| float | floating point limits |
| limits | environmental and integer limits |
| locale | usage according to local customs |
| math | the mathematical functions |
| setjmp | non-local transfer of control |
| signal | signal or interrupt handling |
| stdarg | variable length argument list processing |
| stddef | standard definitions |
| stdio | standard file input and output |
| stdlib | char array conversions, memory management, sundry functions |
| string | char array manipulations |
| time | date and time management |

## B.3  Assert

There is only one function in this library. Its prototype is

**void assert(int expression);**

If *expression* is false, *assert* prints an error message and then calls *abort*. For example

```
/* program b1 - assert */
#include <stdio.h>
#include <assert.h>
#include <stdlib.h>   /* for abort */

void main(void)
{
   int filesOpen = 11;

   assert(filesOpen <= 10);
}
```

results in

```
Assertion failed: filesOpen <= 10   file program.c
Abnormal program termination.
```

being displayed on the screen.

## B.4  Ctype

*ctype* contains the character-processing functions. The argument for each function is an *int* because the storage type must be capable of containing the end-of-file character, *EOF*. The functions listed in Table B.2 return true if their argument meets the stated condition; otherwise, they return false.

**Table B.2**

| Function | Condition |
|---|---|
| int isalnum(int c); | letter or a digit |
| int isalpha(int c); | either an upper-case or a lower-case letter |
| int iscntrl(int c); | control character |
| int isdigit(int c); | decimal (i.e. base 10) digit |
| int isgraph(int c); | printable, but not space |
| int islower(int c); | lower-case letter |
| int isprint(int c); | printable, including space |
| int ispunct(int c); | printable, excluding space, letter and digit |
| int isspace(int c); | space, formfeed, newline, return, tab |
| int isupper(int c); | upper-case letter |

The next two functions convert a character from one case to the other.

**int tolower(int c);** returns the lower case version of c if isupper(c), else returns c

**int toupper(int c);** returns upper-case version of *c* if *islower(c)*, else returns c

## B.5   Errno

*errno.h* defines *errno* in which specific values are automatically placed when a processing error occurs. Functions such as *perror* and *strerror* can be used to translate these values into descriptive error messages to be displayed on the screen – see program b3 in section B.10.1 for example.

## B.6   Float

Any implementation imposes limits on values of type *float*. These limits are described in *float.h*. The prefixes *DBL*, *FLT* and *LDBL* refer to double, float and long double, respectively.

| | |
|---|---|
| **DBL_DIG** | number of decimal digits of precision |
| **DBL_MAX** | largest number of type double |
| **DBL_MIN** | smallest number of type double |

*FLT* or *LDBL* can be used in place of *DBL*, with a corresponding change in the description.

## B.7   Limits

*limits.h* defines the limits for integer values.

| | |
|---|---|
| **INT_MAX** | largest int value |
| **INT_MIN** | smallest int value |
| **LONG_MAX** | largest long int |
| **LONG_MIN** | smallest long int |
| **SHRT_MAX** | largest short int value |
| **SHRT_MIN** | smallest short int value |
| **UINT_MAX** | largest unsigned int |
| **ULONG_MAX** | largest unsigned long int |

## B.8   Math

*math.h* contains the various maths functions which are listed in Table B.3 opposite. The use of *modf* is shown below in program b2.

**Table B.3**

| Function | Returns | Condition/comment |
|---|---|---|
| double exp(double n); | $e^n$ | |
| double ldexp(double m, int n); | $m \times 2^n$ | |
| double log(double n); | $\log_e$ of n | n > 0 |
| double log10(double n); | log10 of n | n > 0 |
| double acos(double n); | inverse cosine | −1.0 < n < 1.0 |
| double asin(double n); | inverse sine | −1.0 < n < 1.0 |
| double atan(double n); | inverse tan | |
| double cos(double n); | cosine of n | |
| double sin(double n); | sine of n | |
| double tan(double n); | tangent of n | |
| double ceil(double n); | smallest integer not less than n. | ceil(17.8) == 18.0 ceil(−17.8) == −17.0 |
| double fabs(double n); | n if n >= 0.0, −n if n < 0.0. | fabs(2.75) == 2.75 fabs(−2.75) == 2.75 |
| double floor(double n); | largest integer not greater than n. | floor(17.8) == 17.0 floor(−17.8) == −18.0 |
| double fmod(double n, double d); | remainder | divides n by d, d > 0.0 remainder same sign as n |
| double pow(double n, double p); | $n^p$ | except if n = 0 and p <= 0 or if n < 0 and y is not an integer |
| double sqrt(double n); | n | n >= 0.0 |
| double modf(double r, double *ip); | | splits r into integer and fraction |

```
/* program b2 - modf */

#include <stdio.h>
#include <math.h>

void main(void)
{
   double fraction, integer;
   double n = 3.1416;
   fraction = modf(n, &integer);
   printf("Integer part = %f, fraction part = %f", integer,
                                               fraction);
}
```

displays Integer part = 3.000000, fraction part = 0.141600.

## B.9   Stddef

*stddef* contains the following definitions

**NULL**    null pointer
**size_t**   type returned by sizeof operator

## B.10   Stdio

A stream represents a file on disk or a device from which data may be read or to which data may be written. *position* is the point in the stream at which the next read or write operation is to take place. *stdio* provides functions which manipulate streams, useful constant definitions known as macros and some type definitions.

| | |
|---|---|
| **FILE** | the file type |
| **fpos_t** | holds current position within a file |
| **BUFSIZ** | default buffer size, typical value = 512 |
| **EOF** | End Of File – returned by some *stdio* functions |
| **FOPEN_MAX** | maximum number of files that can be open at the same time |
| **SEEK_CUR** | seek from current position |
| **SEEK_END** | seek from end of file |
| **SEEK_SET** | seek from beginning of file |
| **stderr** | standard error stream |
| **stdin** | standard input stream |
| **stdout** | standard output stream |

### B.10.1   The Error Functions

Some file processing functions set error and end-of-file indicators, and place a diagnostic integer value in *errno*.

| | |
|---|---|
| **void clearerr(FILE \*stream);** | clears end-of-file and error indicators for *stream* |
| **int feof(FILE \*stream);** | returns non-zero if end of *stream* has been detected, otherwise returns zero. |
| **int ferror(FILE \*stream);** | returns zero if no error has occurred on *stream*, otherwise returns non-zero |
| **void perror(const char \*s);** | prints *s* and a standard error message corresponding to value contained *in errno*. |

For example, program b3 shown below prints

```
junk: No such file or directory.
```

```
/* program b3 - perror */
#include <stdio.h>
void main(void)
{
   char filename[] = "junk";
   FILE *file = fopen(filename, "r");
                                  /* junk does not exist */
   perror(filename);
}
```

## B.10.2   The File Operations

**int fclose(FILE *stream);**   flushes any unwritten data, discards any unread data held in input buffer; returns *EOF* if any errors occur, otherwise returns zero

**int fflush(FILE *stream);**   forces any data held in the buffer to be written into the output stream; returns *EOF* for a write error, otherwise returns zero

**FILE *fopen(const char *file, const char *mode);**   opens file and returns a stream if successful, otherwise returns *NULL*. *mode* strings include

**r**       open text file for reading
**w**       create and open text file for writing
**a**       append i.e. create or open text file for writing at its end
**r+**      open text file for update i.e. reading and writing
**w+**      create text file for update

**rb**      open binary file for reading
**wb**      create and open binary file for writing
**ab**      append i.e. create / open binary file for writing at its end
**r+b**     open binary file for update
        If mode is r+ or r+b (i.e. update) either fflush or a file-positioning function must be called between each read or write.

**int remove(char *file);**   erases the named file, returns non-zero if file cannot be removed

**int rename(const char *oldName, const char *newName);**   changes oldName to newName, returns non-zero if file cannot be renamed

### B.10.3   The Direct File Input–Output Functions

**size_t fread(void *buffer, size_t size, size_t nItems, FILE *stream);**

- reads up to *nItems* items each of *size* bytes from *stream* into *buffer*
- file position is advanced by the number of bytes read
- returns the number of items actually read
- if the number of items actually read is not the requested number of items, *nItems*, *ferror* and *feof* indicates why.

**size_t fwrite(const void *buffer, size_t size, size_t nItems, FILE *stream);**

- writes up to *nItems* each of *size* bytes from *buffer* into *stream*
- file position indicator is increased by amount appropriate to number of bytes written
- returns number of items actually written
- if a write error occurs, items actually written will not be equal to *nItems*.

### B.10.4   The File Positioning Functions

**int fgetpos(FILE *stream, fpos_t *position);**   copies file position for *stream* into *\*position*, returns non-zero on error

**int fseek(FILE *stream, long offset, int beginning);**   sets file position for *stream*; this is the point where the next read or write operation will occur. *offset* is the amount, in bytes, to move from *beginning. beginning* is one of

| | |
|---|---|
| *SEEK_CUR* | the current position |
| *SEEK_END* | the end of the file |
| *SEEK_SET* | the beginning of the file |

For a text stream, *offset* must either be zero or a value returned by *ftell* (in which case beginning must be *SEEK_SET*.
*fseek* returns a non-zero value for an improper seek request.

**int fsetpos(FILE *stream, const fpos_t, *position);**   sets file position indicator at value returned by a previous call to *fgetpos*. Sets *errno* and returns a non-zero value if an error occurs.

**long ftell(FILE *pf);**   returns current position for *stream*, otherwise returns *-1L* and sets *errno*. (If file position cannot be encoded within *long*, use *fgetpos*)

**void rewind(FILE *stream);**   resets file position to beginning of stream

## B.10.5 The Formatted Output Functions

**int fprintf(FILE \*stream, const char \*format, ...);**
> constructs a formatted text and writes it to an output stream; returns the number of characters written, or a value less than zero if an error occurred.

*format* points to a string which contains text and conversion specifications. Each successive conversion specification applies to the next argument in the argument list following format.

A conversion specification has the format

*% flag minFieldWidth .precision modifier conversionCharacter*

The *%* and *conversionCharacter* are compulsory; *flag, minFieldWidth, .precision* and *modifier* are optional.

Flags include

| | |
|---|---|
| **–** | print converted argument left justified within its field (default is right justify) |
| **+** | prefix a signed number with a plus or minus sign |
| **<space>** | minus sign printed if number is negative, otherwise space printed |
| **0** | for numeric conversions, pad with leading zeros to fill field |

*minFieldWidth* – an integer which sets the minimum width of the field in which the converted argument value is to be printed. If the value is too large to fit in its specified field width, then it overflows the field to the right. If an asterisk is used (instead of an integer) then *fprintf* uses the following argument (which must be an *int*) as the field width.

*.precision* – an integer which sets

- the maximum number of characters to the printed from a string or
- the number of digits to be printed after a decimal point or
- the number of significant digits to be printed from an integer.

If an asterisk is used, then *fprintf* uses the following argument (which must be an *int*) as the precision.

*modifier* specifies

| | |
|---|---|
| **h** | *short int* or *unsigned short int* when used before *d, i* or *u* |
| **l** | *long int* or *unsigned long int* when used before *d, i* or *u* |
| **L** | *long double* when used before *e* or *f* |

The common *conversionCharacters* are shown in Table B.4 on the next page.

**Table B.4**

| Character | Argument type converted to |
|---|---|
| c | *int* or *unsigned int* to character |
| d | *int* to signed decimal notation |
| e | *double* to exponential notation d.ddddde+-dd |
| f | *double* to decimal notation +-d.dddddd |
| i | same as *d* |
| p | *void* * print as a pointer in implementation specific notation |
| s | *char* * characters from string until either '\0' reached or precision characters printed |
| u | *int* to *unsigned* decimal notation |
| % | none – print % |

**int printf(const char \*format, argument list);** *printf(...)* is equivalent to *fprintf(stdout, ...);*

### B.10.6  The Formatted Input Functions

**int fscanf(FILE \*stream, const char \*format, ...);** reads characters from stream and uses format to assign values to successive arguments, each of which must be a pointer to an appropriate type; returns (when every conversion in format has been exercised) the number of items scanned and formatted, otherwise returns EOF if a read error has occurred or the end of file has been reached.

*format* points to a string which contains conversion specifications for interpreting the input. Each successive conversion specification applies to the next input field and the result is (usually) placed in the next corresponding argument in the list following format. A format string may contain

- blanks or tabs – these are ignored
- conversion specifications

A conversion specification has the format

*% suppressionCharacter maxFieldWidth modifier conversionCharacter*

The *%* and *conversionCharacter* are compulsory; *suppressionCharacter, maxFieldWidth* and *modifier* are optional.

The suppression character is the asterisk, *. It mean "skip the next input field". An input field is a string of non-white space characters and ends either at the next white-space character or when *maxFieldWidth* characters have been read. A white-space character is either a blank, a tab, a newline or a carriage-return. *fscanf* may (or it may not) read through the newline character. If it does not then the programmer must dispose of the newline character in the input buffer before any subsequent call to *fscanf*, as shown below in program b4.

The modifiers are

h short int or *unsigned short int* when used before *d, i* or *u*
l long int or *unsigned long int* or *double* when used before *d, i, u* or *f*
L long double when used before *e* or *f*

The conversion characters are listed in Table B.5.

**Table B.5**

| Character | Input data; argument type |
|---|---|
| c | characters; char *. The next input characters are placed in the array argument up to the given maxFieldWidth. The default maxFieldWidth is 1. '\0' is not appended to the end of the character sequence held in the array. The normal skip over white-space characters is suppressed. Use %1s to read the next non-white-space character. |
| d | decimal (base 10) integer; int * |
| e | floating point number; float * |
| f | floating point number; float; (for double use lf) |
| i | integer; int *. Integer may be octal or hexadecimal |
| p | pointer value; void * |
| s | string of non-white space characters; char *, receiving array must be sufficiently large, terminating '\0' appended. |
| u | unsigned decimal integer; unsigned int * |
| [...] | matches the longest non-empty string of input characters from the set listed [ and ]; char *. '\0' is added. []...] includes [ in set. |
| [^...] | matches the longest non-empty string of input characters not from the set listed between [ and ]. '\0' is added. |
| % | literal %; no assignment made |

```
/* program b4 - fscanf */

#include <stdio.h>

void main(void)
{
    int i;
    double f;
    char s[BUFSIZ];
```

```
        printf("integer? decimal? string? ");
        fscanf(stdin, "%d%lf%s%*[^\n]", &i, &f, s);
        printf("Integer is %d, decimal is %0.2f, string is %s\n",
                i, f, s);

        printf("And again: integer? decimal? string? ");
        fscanf(stdin, "%d%lf%s%*[^\n]", &i, &f, s);
        printf("Integer is %d, decimal is %0.2f, string is %s\n",
                i, f, s);
    }
```

An example of a program run is

```
integer? decimal? string? 1 2.3 Catastrophe
1 2.3 Catastrophe
And again: integer? decimal? string? 9 9.8 Catastrophic
9 9.8 Catastrophic
```

**int scanf(const char \*format, ...);**   *scanf(...)* is equivalent to fscanf(stdin, ...);

**int sscanf(char \*s, const char \*format, ...);**   *sscanf(s, ...)* is equivalent to *scanf(...);* except that the input is taken from the string *s*.

### B.10.7   The Character Input–Output Functions

**int fgetc(FILE \*stream);**   returns character read from stream and advances file position if no read error has occurred, otherwise returns **EOF** and sets stream's error indicator

**int fgets(char \*string, int n, FILE \*stream);**   reads characters from stream into array string until either *n-1* characters have been read or a newline character has been read or the end-of-file has been reached. It retains the newline character (if there was one) and appends the null character. Returns *NULL* if end of file has been reached or if an error has occurred, otherwise it returns a string.

**int fputc(int c, FILE \*stream);**   writes *c* to *stream* and advances file position. It returns *c* if write successful, otherwise sets error indicator for *stream* and returns *EOF*

**int fputs(char \*s, FILE \*stream);**   writes *s* to *stream*. Terminating null character is not written. *fputs* returns non-negative number if write was successful, otherwise returns *EOF*.

**int getc(FILE \*stream);**   reads a character from *stream*. If no error, returns the character read otherwise sets error indicator and returns *EOF*.

**int getchar(void);**   reads a character from the standard input. If there is no read error, returns character read from standard input, otherwise sets error indicator and returns *EOF.*

**char \*gets(char \*string);**   reads characters from standard input into array *string* until either a newline character or *EOF* character is read; discards the newline or *EOF* character and appends the null character to *string.*

**int putc(int character, FILE \*stream);**   writes *character* to *stream.* If no write error, returns *character* otherwise returns *EOF.*

**int putchar(int character);**   writes character into standard output stream. If character could not be written, error indicator is set and *EOF* is returned, otherwise returns the character written.

**int puts(char \*string);**   replaces the null character at the end of string with the newline character and then writes the result into the standard output stream. *puts* returns a non-negative number if write was successful, otherwise it returns *EOF.*

## B.11   Stdlib

The types defined in *stdlib* are

**div_t**   type of object returned by *div*
**ldiv_t**   type of object returned by *ldiv*

The macros or constants are

**EXIT_FAILURE**   value to indicate failure to execute as expected
**EXIT_SUCCESS**   value to indicate program executed as expected
**RAN_MAX**   largest size of pseudo-random number

The functions are

**int abs(int n);** return absolute value of n

**div_t div(int n, int d);**   divides *n* by *d*, stores quotient in *quot* and remainder in *rem* members of a structure of type *div_t*

**void exit(int status);**   abruptly terminate program execution

**void free(void \*p);**   de-allocate memory previously reserved with *malloc.* Note: *NULL* should be assigned to a *freed* pointer.

**long labs(long n);**   returns absolute value *n*

**ldiv_t ldiv(ling n, long d);**   divides *n* by *d*, stores quotient in *quot* and remainder in *rem* members of a structure of type *ldiv_t*

**void \*malloc(size_t size);**   returns a pointer to a free space in memory large enough to contain an item no larger than *size*

**int rand(void);**   returns a pseudo-random number in the range *0..RAND_MAX* (typically more than 32767)

**void srand(unsigned 'nt seed);**   uses seed to initialise the sequence of pseudo-random numbers generated by *rand*.

**double strtod(const char \*string, char \*\*tail);**   converts string to floating point number. An example of a call is

```
double d;
char string[BUFSIZ];
gets(string);
d = strtod(string, (char **)NULL);
```

**long strtol(const char \*string, char \*\*tail, int base);**   converts string to *long int*. Examples of calls are

```
long m;
int n;
char string[BUFSIZ];
gets(string);
m = strtol(string, (char**), 10);
n = (int)strtol(string, (char**), 10);
```

**unsigned long strtoul(const char \*string, char \*\*tail, int base);**   converts *string* to *unsigned long int*.

**int system(const char \*string);**   passes string to environment (e.g. operating system) for execution. string should be the name of an executable program. Any open files should be closed before system is called.

**void \*bsearch(const void \*key, const void \*array, size_t n, size_t size, int (\*compare)(const void \*arg1, const void \*arg2))**
*bsearch* searches ordered table *array[0]..array[n-1]* for an item that matches *\*key*. The function *compare* must return a negative value if its first argument is less than its second, zero if equal and positive if greater than. *bsearch* returns a pointer to a matching item – if one exists – otherwise it returns *NULL*. Program b5 contains an example of a call to *bsearch*.

```
/* program b5 - binary search */


#include <stdio.h>
#include <stdlib.h>


int intCompare(const void *m, const void *n);


void main(void)
{
   int searchFor = 11;
   int *pResult;
   int numbers[5] = { 2, 4, 6, 8, 10 };

   pResult = (int *)bsearch((void *)&searchFor, (void *)numbers,
               sizeof(numbers) / sizeof(int),
               sizeof(int),
               intCompare);
   if (pResult == NULL)
     printf("Not found\n");
   else
     printf("Item found is %d\n", *pResult);
}


int intCompare(const void *m, const void *n)
{
   int *p = (int *)m;
   int *q = (int *)n;


   if (*p < *q)
     return -1;
   else if (*p == *q)
     return 0;
   else
     return 1;
}
```

**void qsort(void *array, size_t n, size_t size,**
            **int (*compare)(const void *, const void *));** sorts
            *array[0]..array[n-1]* into ascending order. The compare
            function is as described above for *bsearch*.

## B.12   String

**int strcmp(const char \*s, const char \*t);**   compares two strings for equality. Returns -1 if \*s < \*t, 0 if \*s == \*t and 1 if \*s > \*t. The ordering is based on the underlying character representation, e.g. ASCII or EBCDIC.

**int strncmp(const char \*s, const char \*t, int n);**   compares at most the first *n* chars of \*s with \*t for equality. Returns -1 if \*s < \*t, 0 if \*s == \*t and 1 if \*s > \*t.

**char \*strcat(char \*s, const char \*t);**   Adds \*t onto the end of \*s, returns *s*.

**char \*strncat(char \*s, const char \*t, int n);**   adds at most *n* characters from \*t onto \*s, appends '\0'; returns *s*.

**char \*strcpy(char \*s, const char \*t);**   copies \*t into \*s, returns *s*.

**char \*strncpy(char \*s, const char \*t, int n);**   copies at most *n* characters from \*t into \*s. Appends *NULL* to \*s if fewer than *n* characters have been copied. **Warning:** may not append *NULL* to \*s if *n* characters have been copied. Returns *s*.

**char \*strerror(int n);**   return text of a pre-defined error message corresponding to *n*.

**size_t strlen(char const \*s);**   returns length of \*s.

**char \*strchr(const char \*s, char c);**   returns pointer to first occurrence of *c* in \*s – if it is there, otherwise returns *NULL*.

**char \*strstr(const char \*s, const char \*t);**   returns pointer to first occurrence of \*t in \*s – if \*t is in \*s – otherwise returns *NULL*.

**char \*strtok(char \*s, const char \*t);**   breaks string \*s into tokens, each delimited by a character from \*t. *strtok* is called repeatedly. On the first call, it searches \*s for the first character which is not in \*t. If one cannot be found, then *strtok* returns *NULL*. But if one can be found, then it searches \*s for a character which is in \*t; if one is found then it is overwritten by '\0'; a pointer to the rest of \*s is stored and a pointer to the first token is returned. For each subsequent call to *strtok*, the first argument must be *NULL*. *strtok* then looks for subsequent tokens using the pointer to the part \*s not yet tokenised. For example, the following program uses *strtok* to split a full name up into its constituent parts.

```
/* program b6 - strtok */

#include <stdio.h>
#include <string.h>

void main(void)
{
  char tokenSeparators[] = " ";   /* space */
  char name[] = "Ms Audrey Walker-Smith";
  char title[BUFSIZ], firstName[BUFSIZ], secondName[BUFSIZ];

  strcpy(title, strtok(name, tokenSeparators));
  strcpy(firstName, strtok(NULL, tokenSeparators));
  strcpy(secondName, strtok(NULL, tokenSeparators));

  printf(
      "Title is %s, first name is %s, second name is %s\n",
                                title, firstName, secondName);
}
```

When run, program b6 displays

```
Title is Ms, first name is Audrey, second name is Walker-Smith
```

## B.13 Time

Constants or macros

**CLK_TCK**    the number of "ticks" in a second

The types for representing time are listed in Table B.6.

**Table B.6**

| Type | Description |
| --- | --- |
| clock_t | arithmetic type – encodes system time |
| time_t | arithmetic type – encodes time |
| tm | contains calendar time |

The components of a calendar time are held in *struct tm*. The components are given in Table B.7 on the next page.

**Table B.7**

| Member | Description | Range | Comment |
|--------|-------------|-------|---------|
| int tm_sec | seconds after the minute | 0..59 | |
| int tm_min | minutes after the hour | 0..59 | |
| int tm_hour | hours since midnight | 0..23 | 0 == midnight |
| int tm_mday | day of the month | 1..31 | |
| int tm_mon | months since January | 0..11 | 0 == January |
| int tm_year | years since 1900 | | |
| int tm_wday | days since Sunday | 0..6 | 0 == sunday |
| int tm_yday | days since 1 January | 0..365 | |
| int tm_isdt | day-light saving time flag | 0 off, > 0 on | |

The functions are

**char \*asctime(const struct tm \*pt);**   converts calendar time into a string. An example of such as string is *Wed May 31 10:33:15 1995\n\0.*

**clock_t clock(void);**   returns processor time since the start of program execution, or −1 if time not available. *clock()/CLK_TCK* is a time in seconds.

**char \*ctime(const time_t \*pt);**   converts calendar time to local time and returns it as a string format; equivalent to *asctime(localtime(pt)).*

**double difftime(time_t t2, time_t t1);**   returns *t2 - t1* in seconds

**struct tm \*gmtime(const time_t \*pt);**   converts calendar time *\*pt* to Universal Coordinated Time (UCT); returns *NULL* if UCT not available.

**struct tm \*localtime(const time_t \*pt);**   converts calendar time *\*pt* to local time.

**time_t mktime(struct tm \*pt);**   converts local time in structure *\*pt* into calendar time in the same format as used by *time.* Returns the calendar time, or −1 if the time cannot be converted.

**size_t strftime(char \*string, size_t maxChars, const char \*format, const struct tm \*pt);**   formats date and time information from *\*pt* into *string* as defined by format. The string that format points to contains one or more conversion specifications. Each conversion specification is introduced with %. The conversion specifiers are specified in Table B.8.

**time_t time(time_t \*pt);**   returns the current calendar time – if available – otherwise returns -1. If *pt* is not *NULL,* *\*pt* also contains the return value.

**Table B.8**

| Character | Convert to |
|---|---|
| a | abbreviated weekday name |
| A | full weekday name |
| b | abbreviated month name |
| B | full month name |
| c | local data and time representation |
| d | day of the month 01..31 |
| H | hour (24-hour clock) 01..23 |
| I | hour (12-hour clock) 01..12 |
| j | day of the year 01..366 |
| m | month 1..12 |
| M | minute 00..59 |
| p | local equivalent of AM or PM |
| S | second 00..59 |
| U | week of the year 00..53 (Sunday is first day of the week) |
| w | day of the week 0..6 (Sunday is 0) |
| W | day of the week 00.53 (Monday is first day of the week) |
| x | local date representation |
| X | local time representation |
| y | year without century 00..99 |
| Y | year with century |
| Z | time zone, if any |

# Index